SCOTLAND

**CARLISLE &
BORDERLANDS**

Brampton

Carlisle **2**

Wetheral

Wigton

Alston

Garrigill

Maryport

**BASSENTHWAITE
&
BORROWDALE**

Penrith

Cockermouth

931

Vorkington

**WESTERN
LAKES** **6**

7 Keswick **8** **3** Askham

Appleby-in-
Westmorland

Whitehaven

1 Buttermere **2**

Cleator
Moor

950 **9** Patterdale

**ULLSWATER, PENRITH
&
EASTERN FELLS**

Brough

Egremont

899

Grasmere

Gosforth

978 **3** Elterwater

Tebay

**ESKDALE
&
WASDALE**

Coniston

Windermere

4 Ravenglass **5** Seathwaite

1 Bowness-on-
Windermere

Kendal

Sedbergh

Millom

**KENDAL,
WINDERMERE
& KENT ESTUARY**

Ulverston

2

10 **Kirkby
Lonsdale**

Dalton-
in-Furness

Grange-
over-Sands

**Barrow-
in-Furness**

Morecambe

Heysham

Lancaster

6	Walk start point
1	Cycle start point
3	Tour start point

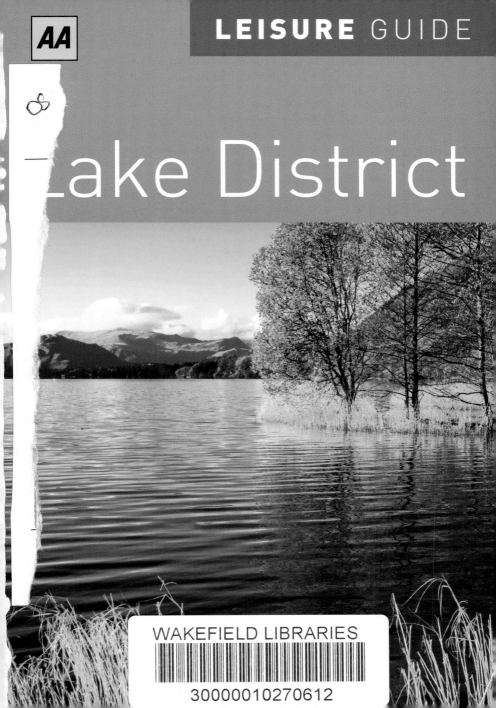

AA

LEISURE GUIDE

Lake District

Authors: Mike Gerrard and John Morrison
Verifier: Chris Bagshaw
Managing Editor: David Popey
Project Management: Bookwork Creative Associates Ltd
Designers: Liz Baldin of Bookwork and Andrew Milne
Picture Library Manager: Ian Little
Picture Research: Alice Earle and Michelle Aylott
Cartography provided by the Mapping Services Department of AA Publishing
Copy-editors: Marilynne Lanng of Bookwork and Pamela Stagg
Internal Repro and Image Manipulation: Jacqueline Street
Production: Rachel Davis

Produced by AA Publishing
© AA Media Limited 2007
Reprinted 2007, 2008
Updated and revised 2010

Published by AA Publishing (a trading name of AA Media Limited, whose registered office is Fanum
House, Basing View, Basingstoke, Hampshire RG21 4EA; registered number 06112600).

 This product includes mapping data licensed from the Ordnance Survey®
with the permission of the Controller of Her Majesty's Stationery Office.
© Crown Copyright 2011. All rights reserved. Licence number 100021153.

ISBN 978-0-7495-6687-6
ISBN 978-0-7495-6700-2 (SS)

A CIP catalogue record for this book is available from the British Library.

The contents of this book are believed correct at the time of printing. Nevertheless, the publishers
cannot be held responsible for any errors or omissions or for changes in the details given in this
book or for the consequences of any reliance on the information it provides. This does not affect your
statutory rights. We have tried to ensure accuracy in this book, but things do change and we would be
grateful if readers would advise us of any inaccuracies they may encounter.

We have taken all reasonable steps to ensure that the walks and cycle rides in this book are safe and
achievable by people with a realistic level of fitness. However, all outdoor activities involve a degree
of risk and the publishers accept no responsibility for any injuries caused to readers while following
these walks and cycle rides. For more advice on walking and cycling in safety see pages 16–17.

Some of the walks and cycle routes may appear in other AA books.

Visit AA Publishing at theAA.com/shop

Printed and bound in China by C&C

A04393

CONTENTS

Welcome to the...

Lake District

You can travel the world seeking beauty in a landscape, but many of the Lake District's 14 million visitors each year believe you will struggle to find somewhere as breathtakingly exquisite as this relatively small corner of northwest England. Our very concepts of what makes a region picturesque were forged here in the late 18th century and we've been returning as gaping tourists ever since.

Here are the craggy mountains, the shining lakes, the cottages to die for, the sylvan woodlands. Here, too, is the graceful osprey, the noble red deer, the impossibly cute red squirrel; even the local Herdwick sheep seem to be part of the rocky pastures they frequent. But for all that, one of Lakeland's most appealing traits is the sheer variety of its landscapes. In the south, the soft Silurian slate supports a series of gentle wooded undulations, giving way on their northern edge to the rough, craggy uplands of Lakeland's volcanic core. This hard stone stands tall – through the awesome power of the glaciers that shaped its valleys and mountains 10,000 years ago – leaving a range of hills higher than any other in England.

These big fells (the word, like so many you'll find here, is Norse in origin) draw hundreds of thousands of walkers and climbers to the heart of the Lake District National Park, but there is plenty of space and a few minutes after escaping from your car you will often find yourself alone in breathtaking countryside. The western and eastern fringes of Lakeland have little in common apart from this sense of solitude. The west is bounded by the Irish Sea and, in some parts, an old industrial belt where lovers of industrial archaeology are perhaps the most satisfied visitors.

In the east, the Lakeland Fells give way to the green uplands of the Eden Valley, a vast unfrequented vale of pretty villages and sparkling rivers. To the north lies the border city of Carlisle, the important wildlife-rich Solway Firth and the World Heritage Site of Hadrian's Wall, stretching away over the watershed into Northumberland. The southern boundary of this delightful region is set by the treacherous shifting sands of Morecambe Bay and, for many holiday-makers from the south, the view of hills across this expanse is the first glimpse of their objective.

The Lake District has much to offer and it is little wonder that it has been a favourite destination for more than 200 years.

SCOTLAND

Langholm

Lockerbie

Dumfries

A7

A74(M)

**CARLISLE &
BORDERLANDS**

A69

Haltwhistle

Hexhar

A69

A689

Brampton

Carlisle **2**

A7

A69

Wetheral

A595

A596

Wigton

M6

Alston

Garrigill

**BASSENTHWAITE
&
BORROWDALE**

A596

Maryport

A595

Penrith

931

A66

Cockermouth **1**

A66

8 **3** Askham

Workington

**WESTERN
LAKES**

A595

6

7 Keswick

A591

2

Appleby-in-
Westmorland

A66

Whitehaven

1

Buttermere

950 **9** Patterdale

**ULLSWATER, PENRITH
&
EASTERN FELLS**

Brough

A66

Cleator
Moor

899

Egremont

978

Grasmere

Tebay

A685

Gosforth

A595

3 Elterwater

A591

A6

M6

Sedbergh

**ESKDALE
&
WASDALE**

Coniston

Windermere

4 Ravenglass

5 Seathwaite

1 Bowness-on-
Windermere

Kendal

**KENDAL,
WINDERMERE
& KENT ESTUARY**

A591

Millom

A595

A590

A590

A590

2

A65

10 Kirkby
Lonsdale

Ulverston

A590

Grange-
over-Sands

Dalton-
in-Furness

Carnforth

Barrow-
in-Furness

Morecambe

M6

Heysham

Lancaster

A65

6	Walk start point
1	Cycle start point
3	Tour start point

Essential Sights

Despite its popularity, the Lake District retains its air of remoteness. Narrow passes, soaring mountains, plunging waterfalls and lakes of every shape and size create a landscape that has inspired poets, writers and artists for more than 200 years. Visit Wordworth's Dove Cottage, gaze across the incomparable Tarn Hows towards Langdale Pikes, steam along the scenic Haverthwaite–Lakeside Railway, negotiate the twists and turns of Hardknott Pass and mingle with mountain climbers and walkers.

1 **Wast Water**
The magnificent view of high fells around the head of Wast Water inspired the Lake District National Park logo, and would probably win many votes for the finest view in England.

2 **Tarn Hows**
Presented to the National Trust in 1930 by the Scott family, Tarn Hows is one of the most visited beauty spots in the Lake District.

3 **Stockghyll Force**
The 70ft (21m) waterfall, Stockghyll Force, is the focus of many lovely walks that can be taken from Ambleside. The waterfall is set in lovely woodland 1 mile (1.6km) to the east of the village.

4 Grasmere
William Wordsworth lived at Grasmere with his sister, wife and young family from 1799 to 1808, writing some of his finest poetry in what he described as 'the loveliest spot that man hath ever found'.

5 Hardknott Roman Fort
Cumbria is criss-crossed by a series of Roman roads. Perhaps the roughest of these highways ran from Ambleside to Ravenglass, where Hardknott lies huddled beneath the road's wildest and highest point. The views from the fort across Eskdale and the high fells are magnificent.

6 Ullswater
The second largest lake in the Lake District, Ullswater offers plenty of watersports, such as windsurfing, cruising and fishing, while the valleys and mountains provide plenty of scenic walks and cycle rides.

7 Bridge at Ashness
The view from here looks north across Derwent Water to the towering peaks of Skiddaw.

8 Rydal Water
Perhaps the most famous visitor to Rydal Water was William Wordsworth, who has a viewpoint named after him.

4

5

6

DAY ONE

Should you be planning a weekend or a short break in the Lake District, these four pages offer a loosely planned itinerary designed to ensure that you make the most of your time, whatever the weather, and see and enjoy the very best that the area has to offer.

Friday Night

Stay in or near Windermere – at Gilpin Lodge Country House Hotel if you can afford it! This delightful hotel, set in 20 acres (8ha) of gardens and woodland, has country-style bedrooms with some beautiful four-poster and brass beds.

Saturday Morning

Cross Windermere using the ferry service from Bowness, then follow the B5285 to visit Beatrix Potter's House, Hill Top, at Near Sawrey. Several of her 'little books' were written in this small 17th-century house.

Continue north on the B5285 to Ambleside, one of the major centres of the Lakes and an excellent place to shop for souvenirs.

If you are in Ambleside on the first Saturday in July, don't miss the rushbearing ceremony that follows in the ancient tradition of strewing the parish church floor with rushes to sweeten and purify the air for festivals and feast days. Today 'rushbearing' is a cross made of rushes or flowers and carried by the children of the parish.

Saturday Lunch

A good place for lunch is the Drunken Duck at Barngates, which is signposted off the B5286 Hawkshead–Ambleside road. It offers a relaxed atmosphere and excellent food.

Saturday Afternoon

Drive north on the A591 for Grasmere and Keswick. Visit Rydal Mount, where William Wordsworth lived from 1813 until his death in 1850. The house is charming as it contains family portraits and many of the Wordsworth's personal possessions, is set in beautiful gardens overlooking Rydal Water.

Continue on the A591 to Grasmere. Explore the village, which has a National Park Information Centre, and then make your way to Dove Cottage and the adjacent buildings – now the Wordsworth Museum and Art Gallery.

Saturday Night

There is plenty of accommodation in Grasmere to suit all pockets, but for something really special stay at the Wordsworth Hotel, set in lovely gardens on Stock Lane, near the church. This outstanding hotel is furnished with fine antiques and serves impressive gourmet meals.

HELM CRAG, GRASMERE

GRASMERE

ULLSWATER

DAY TWO

Our second and final day in the Lakes offers an excellent walk in the morning and a drive that visits a waterfall, the area's second largest lake and its highest pass. If the start of the day is wet then the morning could be spent in Keswick.

Sunday Morning

If it is wet then drive straight to Keswick. It is a natural centre for climbers, walkers and more leisurely tourists alike.

If the weather is fine then it is time to discover the many delights of the Lake District on foot. The Walk on pages 42–43 (2 hours, 4 miles/6.4km) starts at the village of Elterwater, southwest of Grasmere, and leads around the superbly scenic Loughrigg Tarn.

On completing the walk, drive on the A591 to Keswick, passing the waters of Thirlmere on your left and the heights of Helvellyn on your right.

Sunday Lunch

Keswick is the heart of the northern Lake District. You could spend a happy (wet) morning browsing round the town's tempting shops. Visit the Pencil Museum (it's more interesting than you might expect), the Cars of the Stars Motor Museum or discover the unexpected treasures of Keswick Museum and Art Gallery.

When it is time for lunch look out for The Packhorse Inn in the town centre, an attractive and comfortable pub with good food that welcomes children.

Sunday Afternoon

After lunch leave Keswick on the A66 travelling east. Turn right on to the A5091 heading down towards Aira Force (in the care of the National Trust), a series of splendid waterfalls in a spectacular gorge, with an arboretum, a café and a landscaped Victorian park.

Leave the car park and travel south on the A592 along the western shore of Ullswater (the second largest lake in the Lake District), passing through the popular tourist-packed villages of Glenridding and Patterdale.

Continue on the A592 to travel along the spectacular Kirkstone Pass (the highest road pass in the Lake District) to return to Windermere.

Just before reaching Windermere detour through the village of Troutbeck and visit Townend, a 17th-century wealthy yeoman farmer's house.

Route facts

MINIMUM TIME The time stated for completing each route is the estimated minimum time that a reasonably fit family group of walkers or cyclists would take to complete the circuit. This does not allow for rest or refreshment stops.

OS MAP Each route is shown on a map. However, some detail is lost because of the restrictions imposed by scale, so for this reason, we recommend that you use the maps in conjunction with a more detailed Ordnance Survey map. The relevant map for each walk or cycle ride is listed.

START This indicates the start location and parking area. This is a six-figure grid reference prefixed by two letters showing which 62.5-mile (100km) square of the National Grid it refers to. You'll find more information on grid references on most Ordnance Survey maps.

CYCLE HIRE We list, within reason, the nearest cycle hire shop/centre.

❶ Here we highlight any potential difficulties or dangers along the cycle ride or walk. If a particular route is suitable for older, fitter children we say so here. Also, we give guidelines of a route's suitability for younger children, for example the symbol 8+ indicates that the route can probably be attempted by children aged 8 years and above.

Walks & Cycle Rides

Each walk and cycle ride has a panel giving information for the walker and cyclist, including the distance, terrain, nature of the paths, and where to park your car.

WALKING

All of the walks are suitable for families, but less experienced family groups, especially those with younger children, should try the shorter walks. Route finding is usually straightforward, but the maps are for guidance only and we recommend that you always take the relevant Ordnance Survey map with you.

Risks

Although each walk has been researched with a view to minimising any risks, no walk in the countryside can be considered to be completely free from risk. Walking in the outdoors will always require a degree of common sense and judgement to ensure that it is as safe as possible, especially for young children.

• Be particularly careful on cliff paths and in upland terrain, where the consequences of a slip can be serious.

• Remember to check tidal conditions before walking on the seashore.

• Some sections of route are by, or cross, busy roads.

Remember traffic is a danger even on minor country lanes.

• Be careful around farmyard machinery and livestock.

• Be prepared for the consequences of changes in the weather and check the forecast before you set out.

• Ensure the whole family is properly equipped, wearing suitable clothing and a good pair of boots or sturdy walking shoes. Take waterproof clothing with you and a torch if you are walking in the winter months.

• Remember the weather can change quickly at any time of the year, and in moorland and heathland areas, mist and fog can make route-finding much harder. In summer, take account of the heat and sun by wearing a hat, sunscreen and carrying enough water.

• On walks away from centres of population you should carry a mobile phone, whistle and, if possible, a survival bag. If you do have an accident requiring emergency services, make a note of your position as accurately as possible and dial 999 (112 on a mobile).

CYCLING

In devising the cycle rides in this guide, every effort has been made to use designated cycle paths, or to link them with quiet country lanes and waymarked byways and bridleways. In a few cases, some fairly busy B-roads have been used to join up with quieter routes.

Rules of the road

• Ride in single file on narrow and busy roads.
• Be alert, look and listen for traffic, especially on narrow lanes and blind bends and be extra careful when descending steep hills, as loose gravel or a poor road surface can lead to an accident.
• In wet weather make sure that you keep an appropriate distance between you and other riders.
• Make sure you indicate your intentions clearly.
• Brush up on *The Highway Code* before venturing out onto the road.

Off-road safety code of conduct

• Only ride where you know it is legal to do so. Cyclists are not allowed to cycle on public footpaths (yellow waymarkers). The only 'rights of way' open to cyclists are bridleways (blue markers) and unsurfaced tracks, known as byways, which are open to all traffic and waymarked in red.
• Canal tow paths: you need a permit to cycle on some stretches of tow path (www.waterscape.com). Remember that access paths can be steep and slippery so always push your bike under low bridges and by locks.
• Always yield to walkers and horses, giving adequate warning of your approach.
• Don't expect to cycle at high speeds.
• Keep to the main trail to avoid any unnecessary erosion to the area beside the trail and to prevent skidding, especially in wet weather conditions.
• Remember to follow the Country Code.

Preparing your bicycle

Check the wheels, tyres, brakes and cables. Lubricate hubs, pedals, gear mechanisms and cables. Make sure you have a pump, a bell, a rear rack to carry panniers and a set of lights.

Equipment

• A cycling helmet provides essential protection.
• Make sure you are visible to other road users, by wearing light-coloured or luminous clothing in daylight and sashes or reflective strips in failing light and darkness.
• Take extra clothes with you, depending on the season, and a wind/waterproof jacket.
• Carry a basic tool kit, a pump, a strong lock and a first aid kit.
• Always carry enough water for your outing.

Walk Map Legend

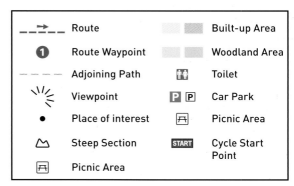

---→	Route	(shaded)	Built-up Area
①	Route Waypoint	(shaded)	Woodland Area
– – –	Adjoining Path	🚻	Toilet
⚡	Viewpoint	P P	Car Park
●	Place of interest	🅿	Picnic Area
⌂	Steep Section	START	Cycle Start Point
🅿	Picnic Area		

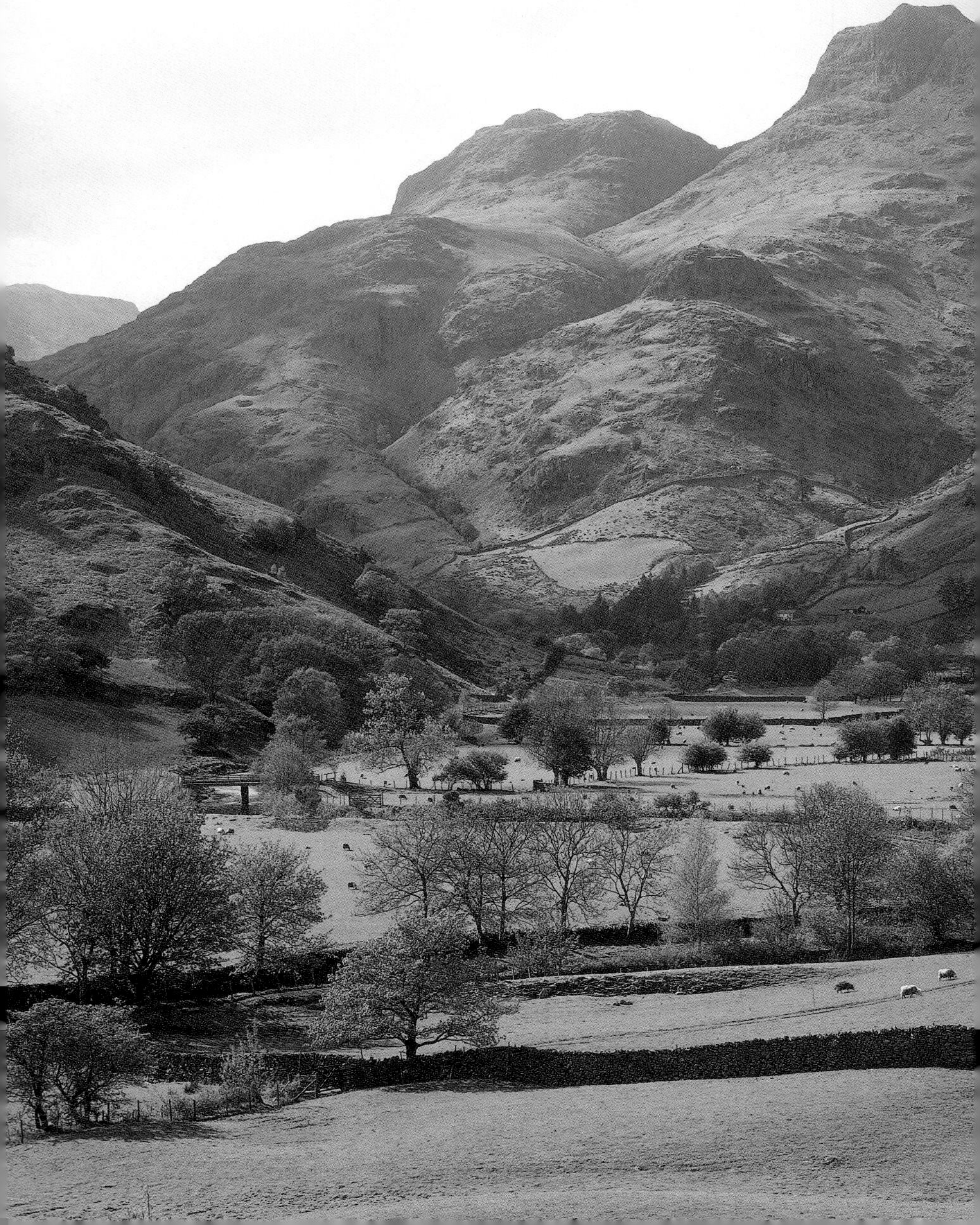

Kendal, Windermere & Kent Estuary

There are fascinating towns and villages in south Lakeland, some looking out over Morecambe Bay, that are all too often overlooked by visitors. The landscape here, generally greener and more intimate in character than the higher Lakeland hills, offers delightful walking country in which you can find the 'quiet recreation' enshrined in the philosophy of the National Park.

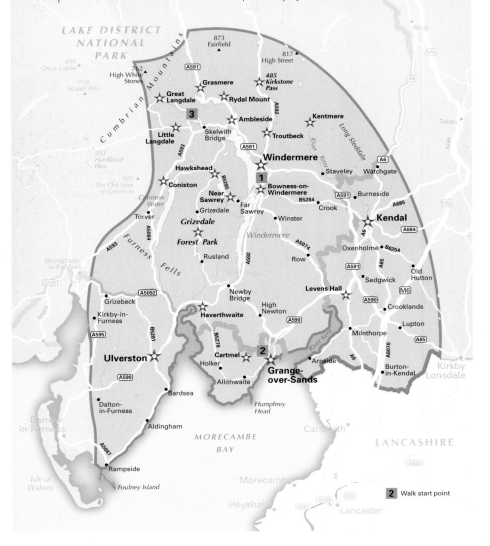

Unmissable attractions

At Bowness Bay, you can hire dinghies or take a more leisurely cruise. Picturesquely situated at its head is Ambleside, popularised by the Lakeland poets. To the east, Kirkstone Pass is the highest road in the Lake District and passes through magnificent scenery. Literary pilgrims will be drawn to Grasmere since Wordsworth produced some of his finest poetry there. To the west, lie the beautiful Langdale valleys and the distinctive Langdale Pikes for those looking for challenging climbs, scrambles, as well as lowland rambles. Coniston Water enjoys a superb setting overlooked by the bulk of the Old Man of Coniston and Kendal, with its steep streets of busy shops, remains the essential standby for walkers.

1

1 Windermere
Windermere is the largest natural freshwater lake in England. Boating and sailing facilities on the lake are excellent.

2 Dove Cottage, Grasmere
William Wordsworth found this little house while on a walking tour of the Lake District. It is a must-see for poetry lovers.

3 Little Langdale
A predominance of oak and deciduous woodlands cloak the valley flanks and bottom. The Langdale Pikes form an imposing backdrop.

AMBLESIDE MAP REF NY3704

Lying at the northern tip of Windermere lake, Ambleside is a convenient base for touring the central Lakes, with Grasmere and the Langdale valleys just a short drive away. The town has adopted this role with gusto; it seems that every other shop sells walking boots and outdoor clothing.

The Romans first saw the strategic potential of this site, and built a fort they called Galava close to where the rivers Brathay and Rothay combine and flow into Windermere. Many centuries later, during Queen Victoria's reign, the town gained fame and prosperity through the steady growth of tourism.

Ambleside won its market charter in 1650, and a few buildings – including a watermill – survive from this time. However, the best-known and most photographed building in Ambleside is also the smallest: Bridge House is built on a little bridge that spans the beck of Stock Ghyll. Thought to have been built by the owners of Ambleside Hall, perhaps as a folly or apple store, Bridge House, once home to a family with six children, now serves as a diminutive National Trust shop.

■ Visit

THE ARMITT COLLECTION

Ambleside's museum was founded as a library in 1909 by the Armitt sisters. It's now a fine small museum illustrating the life and work of writers and artists such as John Ruskin, Beatrix Potter and the Collingwoods. The collection includes most of Beatrix Potter's scientific illustrations as well as pictures by artists such as William Green and J B Pyne.

It is just a short walk from the centre of Ambleside to the lake at Waterhead. Like a Bowness Bay in miniature, with a short stretch of beach, rowing boats for hire and ever-hungry ducks, Waterhead is a favourite holiday spot. The steamers *Swan*, *Tern* and *Teal* call in at Waterhead on their round-the-lake cruises.

A walk in the opposite direction, following Stock Ghyll through lovely woodland, will bring you to Stockghyll Force, an entrancing waterfall. 'Force' is a corruption of 'foss', the old Norse word for waterfall.

CARTMEL MAP REF SD3878

First-time visitors will wonder why a village as small as Cartmel should be blessed with such a large and magnificent church. In the 12th century when Cartmel (along with Carlisle and Lanercost) was chosen as the site for an Augustinian priory, the original endowment stipulated that local people should always have the right to worship in the priory church. When the monastery itself was disbanded by the Dissolution in 1536–37, the priory church was fortunately saved.

Much of the stone from the priory was re-used to build what is now the village of Cartmel, and the only other tangible relic of monastic times is the gatehouse (now a private residence in the care of the National Trust) that forms one side of the little market square. The stepped market cross stands near by, but the markets themselves are long gone. The Cartmel of today is a pretty little village, worth exploring in its own right as well as for its gem of a church.

To the south of the village is Holker Hall, the home of the Cavendish family; allow plenty of time for your visit because there is a lot to see. The Hall itself retains the atmosphere of a family home, not least because you are free to explore the rooms unhindered by ropes and barriers. The 25 acres (10ha) of formal gardens and woodland are justifiably renowned. Features to look for include the Ice House, where ice was stored in Victorian times to serve the great house. Look out for the rhododendrons and the great Holker Lime, one of the largest trees of its kind in Britain. Planted in the 17th century it is 26 feet (7.9m) in circumference.

CONISTON   MAP REF SD3097

Overlooked by the bulk of the Old Man of Coniston, 2,627 feet (801m), and near the northern tip of Coniston Water, the village enjoys a superb setting. A little off the beaten track, Coniston caters best for those who want to explore the magnificent range of peaks that rise up behind the little grey town.

It was these mountains, and the mineral wealth they yielded, that created the village of Coniston. While copper had been mined in this area since the Roman occupation, the industry grew most rapidly during the 18th and 19th centuries and the village expanded accordingly. The story of copper mining, slate quarrying and farming, as well as the lives of celebrities such as John Ruskin, Arthur Ransome and Donald Campbell, are told in the Ruskin Museum. Situated in the village since 1901, it has been recently revitalised.

■ Visit

DARING EXPLOITS
The collection of full-size replicas of their futuristic cars and boats at the Lakeland Motor Museum, at Backbarrow near Newby Bridge, incorporates an exhibition featuring the record-breaking exploits of the remarkable Campbells, Sir Malcolm (1885–1948) and his son Donald (1921–67), whose adventures on land and water thrilled the world.

A short stroll from the centre of Coniston brings you to the shore of the lake where a public slipway allows the launching of boats (no powered craft); sailing dinghies and rowing boats can be hired by the hour.

Few houses enjoy a more beautiful setting than Brantwood, in an estate on the eastern shore of the lake. From 1872 to 1900 this was the home of John Ruskin, artist, poet and social reformer, who became the most influential and controversial art critic of his time. The grounds are an attraction in their own right, and the house is filled with many of Ruskin's drawings, watercolours and other items recalling the man whose ideas influenced such intellectual giants as Mahatma Gandhi and Leo Tolstoy. Ruskin is buried in Coniston churchyard.

Tarn Hows, one of the most-visited beauty spots in the Lakes, is just a short drive from Coniston off the B5285 Hawkshead road. Just yards from the National Trust car park, you can gaze across the tarn, studded with islands, surrounded by gorgeous conifer woodland and the most beautiful backdrop of rolling hills.

GRANGE-OVER-SANDS

MAP REF SD4077

Looking out over Morecambe Bay is the charming little resort of Grange-over-Sands, with its ornamental gardens, 1-mile-long (1.6km) promenade and relaxed ambience.

Thanks to the Gulf Stream, Grange enjoys a congenially mild climate, a factor which helps to explain why so many people find the town a pleasant place in which to spend their retirement years. Springtime is reckoned to be warmer in Grange than anywhere else in the north. Green-fingered gardeners are encouraged by the climate, and plants grow here that would be unlikely to survive elsewhere on the west coast.

GRASMERE MAP REF NY3307

The village of Grasmere is central, geographically and historically, to the Lake District. Set in a valley surrounded by hills, and a short stroll from Grasmere lake, the village is a gem.

Literary pilgrims have flocked to Grasmere since the days when William Wordsworth's 'plain living and high thinking' produced some of the finest romantic poetry. It was during a walking tour of the Lake District, with his lifelong friend Samuel Taylor Coleridge, that Wordsworth first spied the little house that would become his home for eight of his most productive years.

Despite its size, the house came to be filled with the artistic luminaries of the day, and it was here, between 1799 and 1808, that he composed some of his best-known poems. Previously an inn (The Dove and Olive Branch),

Wordsworth knew the house as Town End. It was years later, after the poet's death, that it was christened Dove Cottage. The house is open to the public, and an adjacent coach house has been converted into the Wordsworth Museum. The attached Jerwood Centre is for academic studies. It was opened in 2005 and has won awards for architecture.

By the time Wordsworth's wife, Mary, was expecting their fourth child, Dove Cottage was becoming too small. The family moved first to Allan Bank and the Rectory (both in Grasmere, and both now private homes), before making one last move to Rydal Mount.

GRIZEDALE FOREST

MAP REF SD3394

The Grizedale estate, situated between the lakes of Coniston Water and Windermere, was the first forest owned by the Forestry Commission to actively encourage a variety of recreational activities. The forest was opened to the public in the 1960s, and Grizedale is now the largest forest in the Lake District.

The Grizedale Forest combines two roles: woodland recreation and the commercial production of timber. Your first stop should be the visitor centre where you can get a guide to the forest's many waymarked trails.

An imaginative initiative brought art into the forest. Sculptors were regularly sponsored to create artworks in woodland settings; there are now more than 80 original sculptures, to be found nestling among the trees or standing on grassy hilltops.

Brant Fell at Bowness-on-Windermere

Bowness-on-Windermere is the main gateway and access point for Windermere, England's largest natural lake. This walk takes you from the lake's shores to high ground above the bustling town. With relatively little effort you can crest the heights of Brant Fell and enjoy wonderful views over Windermere and the Coniston fells.

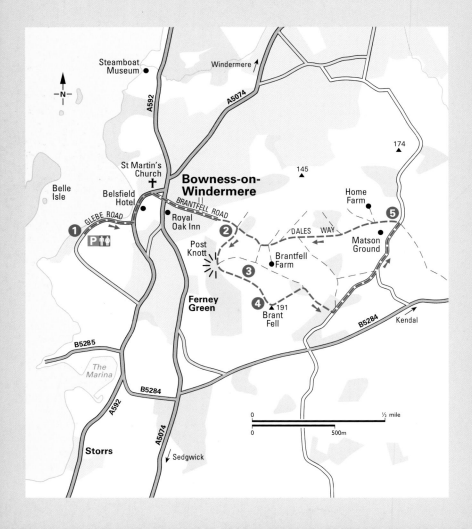

Route Directions

1 Take Glebe Road into Bowness town. Swing left and, opposite the steamer pier, go right over the main Windermere road and then turn left. Opposite the impressive St Martin's Church turn right to ascend the little street of St Martins Hill. Cross the Kendal road to climb Brantfell Road directly above. At the head of the road a little iron gate leads on to the Dales Way, a grassy and stony path which climbs directly up the hillside. Continue to a kissing gate by the wood, leading on to a lane.

2 Pass through the kissing gate and turn right, signposted 'Post Knott', to follow the stony lane. Continue on the lane rising through the woods until it crests a height near the flat circular top of Post Knott. Bear left and make the short ascent to the summit. The view from here was once exceptional but is now obscured by trees. Retrace a few steps back to the track then bear right to find a kissing gate leading out of the wood on to the open hillside.

3 Beyond the kissing gate take the grassy path, rising to a rocky shoulder. Cross the shoulder and first descend,

then ascend to a ladder stile in the top corner of the field by some fir trees. Cross the stile then bear right to ascend directly up the open grassy flanks of Brant Fell to its rocky summit.

4 Go left (northeast) from the top of the fell, following a line of cairns down to a kissing gate. Descend through a young plantation to a second gate and a track. Turn right and follow the track to a stile and gate leading out to a road. Turn left along the road and continue left at the junction, to pass Matson Ground. Immediately beyond is a kissing gate on the left, waymarked for the Dales Way.

5 Go through the kissing gate and continue down the path to cross a track and pass through a kissing gate into another field. Keep along the track beneath the trees and beside a new pond, until the path swings left to emerge through a kissing gate on to a surfaced drive. Go right along the drive for 30yds (27m) until the path veers off left through the trees to follow the fence. An iron gate leads into a field. Follow the grassy path, first descending and then rising to an iron gate in the corner of the field. Continue to join a grassy track and go through

the kissing gate. Cross the surfaced drive of Brantfell Farm and keep straight on to another kissing gate leading into a field. Follow the path, parallel to the wall, descending the hill to intercept a track, via a kissing gate, and regain Point 2. Retrace your steps back to Glebe Road.

Route facts

DISTANCE/TIME 3.5 miles (5.7km) 1h30

MAP OS Explorer OL7 The English Lakes (SE)

START Pay-and-display car park on Glebe Road above lake, Bowness-on-Windermere; grid ref:SD 398966

TRACKS Pavement, road, stony tracks, grassy paths, 2 stiles

GETTING TO THE START Bowness-on-Windermere is on the A592 just south of Windermere town, and the A591 Kendal-to-Ambleside road. In Bowness, turn left just before the steamer terminal into Glebe Road, where the main car parks are located.

THE PUB Royal Oak Inn, Bowness-on-Windermere. Tel: 01539 443970

❶ Care needed with traffic on busy streets at the start and finish. Suitability: children 6+

Over Hampsfell from Grange-over-Sands

A walk through woods, gardens and over open fell above a charming seaside resort which retains a refined air of quiet dignity. The town has many fine and interesting buildings and its ornamental gardens, complete with ponds, provide suitable solitude in which to relax and enjoy a picnic.

Route Directions

1 Join the main road through Grange and go right (heading north), to pass the ornamental gardens. Cross the road and continue along the pavement to the roundabout. Go left along Windermere Road rising to round the bend, and find steps

up to a squeeze stile on the left, signed 'Routon Well/Hampsfield'.

2 Take the path rising through Eggerslack Wood. Cross directly over a surfaced track and continue to pass a house on the left. Steps lead on to a track. Cross this diagonally to follow a track, signed 'Hampsfell'. The track zig-zags to the right (with a house to the left) and continues up through the woods to a stile over the wall.

3 Cross the stile to leave the wood and follow the path directly up the hillside. Pass sections of limestone pavement and little craggy outcrops until the path levels and bears left to a stile over a stone wall. Cross the stile and go right along the wall. Continue in the same direction, following a grassy track, to pass ancient stone cairns and up to the obvious square tower landmark of the Hospice of Hampsfell.

4 Leave the tower, head south and follow the path over the edge of a little limestone escarpment (take care here). Continue over another escarpment and descend to find a stile over the wall. Descend to the bottom of the dip and rise directly up the

green hill beyond. Cross over the top and descend to find a stile over the wall. Although the path bears diagonally left at this point it is usual to continue directly to the little cairn marking Fell End, with fine views over the estuary. Turn sharp left and descend to pick up a grassy track leading left round a little valley of thorn bushes to a gate leading out on to a road.

5 Cross the road, take the squeeze stile and descend diagonally left across the field to a gate on to a road by the front door of Springbank Cottage. Descend the surfaced track to enter a farmyard and continue left over a stone stile. Go over the hill, following the path that is parallel to the wall and then take the stile into a narrow ginnel. Follow this down, with a high garden wall to the right, round the corner and descend to a junction of roads. Go left on a private road/public footpath, and then bear right at the fork. At the next junction turn right to descend the track and at the following junction go left down Charney Well Lane. When you get to another junction, turn left below the woods of Eden Mount to a junction with Hampsfell Road near the bottom of the hill and

turn right. At the junction with a larger road go left (toilets to the right) and pass the church before descending to pass the clock tower and junction with the main road (B5277). Go left and then right to the car park.

Route facts

DISTANCE/TIME 4 miles (6.4km) 2h

MAP OS Explorer OL7 The English Lakes (SE)

START Car park below road and tourist office, central Grange; grid ref: SD 410780

TRACKS Paths and tracks, can be muddy in places, 7 stiles

GETTING TO THE START
Grange-over-Sands is on the coast, south of Newby Bridge. Take the B5277 into the town. Just after the railway station keep left and follow the main street until signs point to a parking area down a lane on the left, below the Commodore Inn.

THE PUB The Lancastrian, Grange-over-Sands, near the start of the route. Tel: 01539 532455

❶ Care needed with traffic on busy streets at the start and finish. Suitability: children 6+

HAVERTHWAITE MAP REF SD3483

Haverthwaite, beyond the southern tip of Windermere, is the southern terminus of the Lakeside and Haverthwaite Railway. Originally a branch of the Furness Railway, the line used to carry goods and passengers from Ulverston to connect with the Windermere steamers at Lakeside. Four passenger steamers began service in 1850; trains began running 20 years later. Passenger numbers peaked before the First World War, but the story, subsequently, was sadly one of decline, curtailed services and finally, in 1967, closure.

A group of rail enthusiasts fought to buy the branch line and re-open it as a recreational line, using steam-hauled trains. Despite many setbacks they succeeded in taking over the 3.5-mile (5.6km) stretch of line between Haverthwaite and Lakeside. The proud re-opening came in 1973; since then a full service has been maintained. As in the railway's heyday, the scenic journey can be combined with a leisurely cruise on Windermere.

■ Activity

FELL FOOT PARK

Fell Foot Park (National Trust) offers one of the few sites on Windermere's eastern shore with public access to the water. This 18-acre (7ha) park offers safe bathing, boats for hire and space to spread a picnic blanket. A ferry runs between Fell Foot Park and Lakeside, where you will find the terminus of the restored railway and steamer berth as well as the Aquarium of the Lakes with its imaginative naturalistic displays of water and bird life in rivers, lakes and nearby Morecambe Bay.

Newby Bridge marks the southern limit of the lake, where it drains into the River Leven. The hotel, by the bridge, with tables overlooking the river, is an ideal spot to while away an idle hour. Two miles (3.2km) from Newby Bridge is Stott Park Bobbin Mill. The 1835 building is an evocative reminder of a local industry that produced bobbins for the clattering textile mills of Lancashire.

HAWKSHEAD MAP REF SD3598

Achingly picturesque, Hawkshead has suffered in recent years from the influx of visitors. Though a large car park now ensures the narrow streets comprise a car-free zone, this is no place to be on a busy bank holiday. However, the village has retained much of the charm that first endeared it to the young William Wordsworth, when, between 1779 and 1787, he was a pupil at the Grammar School and lodged with Ann Tyson.

It was during his schooldays that Wordsworth developed the passion for the Lakeland hills that fuelled so much of his poetry. Ann Tyson's cottage still stands, as does the school (you can see the desk on which the young schoolboy carved his name).

Hawkshead is an intriguing maze of tiny thoroughfares, alleyways and courtyards. The whitewashed houses – many 17th-century – never suffered at the hands of an unimaginative town planner, and exhibit an architectural anarchy that merely adds to the charm of the village. The 15th-century parish church boasts wall frescoes, but its main charm is its position on a knoll overlooking the village.

A more recent attraction is the National Trust's Beatrix Potter Gallery, in the middle of the village, where you will find displays of Beatrix's original drawings, and information about her life as author, artist, farmer and pioneer of the conservation movement.

Hawkshead was once an important market town serving a wide area, much of it owned by the monks of Furness Abbey. Only one building now remains from monastic times: the sturdy little courthouse, just north of the village.

KENDAL MAP REF SD5192

For motorists coming from the M6, the first sight of Kendal, in the valley below, means that the Lakes are 'only just round the corner'. Though some motorists take the bypass, impatient to reach Bowness or Windermere, others prefer to see what Kendal has to offer. The one-way traffic system can be frustrating so it's better to explore on foot, and investigate Kendal's numerous 'yards' or alleyways.

Catherine Parr, sixth wife of Henry VIII, was born in Kendal Castle, which enjoys a splendid view over the town. The view still repays the climb, though the castle itself is in ruins.

Near the parish church is Abbot Hall. This elegant Georgian house is now an equally elegant art gallery, showing works by the many artists – including Ruskin and Constable – who were inspired by the Lakeland landscape. The Museum of Lakeland Life and Industry, also at Abbot Hall, brings recent history to life, with reconstructed shops, room settings and a farming

THE QUAKER TAPESTRY
Inside the Friend's Meeting House in Kendal, 77 beautifully embroidered panels, the work of 4,000 men, women and children from 15 countries, illustrate the social history of the Quaker Movement.

display. The study of Arthur Ransome, author of *Swallows and Amazons* and many other children's books, has been painstakingly recreated.

At the opposite end of town, close to the railway station, the Kendal Museum has fascinating displays of geology, archaeology and natural and social history, based on the collection of 'curiosities' first exhibited by William Todhunter in 1796. He charged 'one shilling per person; children and servants 6d each'. There are displays of wildlife, both local and global (though the case full of iridescent humming birds seems gross by today's standards).

One of Kendal's best-known adopted sons was Alfred Wainwright (1907–91), whose seven handwritten guides to the Lakeland hills became classics in his own lifetime. You can see Wainwright's little office in Kendal Museum, where he held the post of honorary curator for many years. A hand-drawn map reveals that his interests were already in place at the tender age of ten. However, it wasn't until he was 45 that he began the mammoth task of writing his Pictorial Guides, which were indispensable reading for many years to come. Other books about his beloved North Country followed, until his death in 1991.

KENTMERE   MAP REF NX4603

The valley of Kentmere begins at Staveley, just off the A591 between Kendal and Windermere. From Staveley the road meanders prettily along the valley bottom, northwards, never too far from the infant River Kent (which later splits the town of Kendal in two) before coming to a halt at the charming little village of Kentmere. The village church, St Cuthbert's, has a bronze memorial to Bernard Gilpin, who was born at Kentmere Hall in 1517 and eventually became Archdeacon of Durham Cathedral. From Kentmere you can continue to explore the head of the valley on foot, or take footpaths 'over the top' into either the Troutbeck valley or the remote upper reaches of Longsleddale. Be warned, you need to arrive early in the village to find a parking space at busy times.

KIRKSTONE PASS

MAP REF NY4008

Kirkstone Pass is, at a maximum of 1,489 feet (454m), the highest road in the Lake District, as well as one of the most spectacular. Charabancs used to labour up the long haul, from either Ambleside or Troutbeck; the Kirkstone Inn, where these roads converge, would have been a welcome sight for passengers. The pub, one of the most isolated in Cumbria, is still a popular halt; it takes its name from the nearby Kirk Stone, which resembles a church steeple.

The Kirkstone Pass continues through some magnificent mountain scenery, before dropping down, past Brothers Water, into Patterdale.

THE LANGDALES

MAP REF NY3006/3103

The Langdales are considered to be two of the most beautiful valleys in the Lake District. They are no secret, as you will find if you try to make the circular drive around Great Langdale and Little Langdale on a weekend in summer. The road is very narrow; it's best to park at Skelwith Bridge or Elterwater, and tackle the area on foot. There are climbs and scrambles here to challenge the sure-footed, as well as lowland rambles if you just want to enjoy the view.

At Skelwith Bridge, where the B5343 Langdale road branches off from the A593, is Skelwith Force. The path to the waterfall continues to Elter Water, where you can enjoy one of the many views that seems to typify the Lake District – the distinctive silhouette of the Langdale Pikes. The twin humps of Harrison Stickle (2,415 feet/736m) and Pike of Stickle (2,323 feet/708m) are glimpsed from many different points.

Beyond the village of Chapel Stile, the Great Langdale valley opens up in spectacular fashion. The valley floor is divided up by stone walls, dotted with farmsteads and surrounded by a frieze of mountain peaks. The valley road meanders past the Old Dungeon Ghyll Hotel. After a steep climb the road drops, with views of Blea Tarn, into the Little Langdale valley. Though not as stunning as the main valley, it is delightful and has good footpaths. It is from Little Langdale that a minor road branches west, to become first Wrynose Pass and then Hardknott Pass – exciting driving if your brakes are in good order!

■ Activity

WATER POWER

A popular walk in the Great Langdale valley begins at the New Dungeon Ghyll Hotel, and passes the foaming white water of Dungeon Ghyll Force before climbing steeply uphill by Stickle Ghyll waterfalls. A surprise awaits at the top – the still waters of the beautiful Stickle Tarn, with the vertiginous cliff-face of Pavey Ark behind.

■ Insight

GHOSTLY LEVENS HALL

Levens Hall has more than its share of ghosts. One is the Grey Lady, able to walk straight through walls, and supposed to be the ghost of a gypsy woman who was refused refreshment at the Hall. She put a curse on the house, saying that no male would inherit Levens Hall until the River Kent ceased to flow and a white deer was seen in the park. The hall did indeed pass through the female line until the birth of Alan Desmond Bagot in 1896 – an event that coincided with the river freezing over and the appearance of a white fawn.

As fine as the house is, the most famous feature is outdoors. In 1688 Levens came into the possession of Colonel James Grahme [sic], who had a passion for gardening. He engaged Monsieur Beaumont to 'improve' on nature by creating a topiary garden, in which yew trees were clipped into a variety of shapes – resembling nothing so much as a surreal set of chess pieces. The designs we see today, probably the finest examples in the country, are much as they were designed three centuries ago.

Just a mile (1.6km) north of Levens Hall is Sizergh Castle, home of the Strickland family since 1239 and now owned by the National Trust. This is another building whose nucleus was a defensive pele tower that dates from the aggressive Scottish incursions of the 14th century. The house has many fine features and the gardens, with lovely views over the lower Lakeland fells, are well worth exploring.

LEVENS HALL   MAP REF SD4984

Levens Hall, just south of Kendal, is well worth a visit. The beginnings of the Hall can be traced back to a 14th-century pele tower. Typically square, with thick walls and narrow windows, the towers allowed the wealthier landowners to protect their families, livestock and servants in times of danger. The grim medieval tower at Levens was later incorporated into a more elaborate Elizabethan building to create a comfortable family home. Levens Hall has passed through many hands, and now belongs to the Bagot family.

NEAR SAWREY   MAP REF SD3795

Beatrix Potter first came here on holiday in 1896, fell in love with the place and used the royalties from her first book, *The Tale of Peter Rabbit* (1901), to buy Hill Top. It was in this unpretentious little 17th-century farmhouse that she wrote many of the books that have delighted readers throughout the world.

The success of the books allowed Beatrix Potter to buy up farms and land: all her properties were bequeathed, on her death in 1943, to the National Trust. Her will decreed that Hill Top should remain exactly as she had known it.

Visitors will recognise details from the pictures in her books and even the adjacent inn, the Tower Bank Arms, will be familiar to readers of *The Tale of Jemima Puddleduck* (1908). Disregard its unprepossessing exterior; Hill Top is chock full of Beatrix Potter memorabilia, including original drawings.

Hill Top is so popular that it is best avoided at peak holiday times. The Beatrix Potter Gallery at Hawkshead and The World of Beatrix Potter at Bowness hold lots of interest for 'Potterphiles'.

RYDAL MOUNT   MAP REF NY3606

By the time William Wordsworth and his family had moved to Rydal Mount, their home until the poet's death, he had already written most of the poems on which his considerable reputation now rests. The house was bought in 1969 by Mary Henderson, the poet's great great granddaughter and opened to the public the following year displaying mementoes of a life devoted to literature.

While living in Rydal Mount, William Wordsworth became Distributor of Stamps for Westmorland. More propitiously he accepted the post of Poet Laureate at the age of 73, on the strict condition that he would not be have to compose verse on demand.

In the gardens of Rydal Mount, designed by Wordsworth himself, are the terrace and shelter where many of his later poems were composed. If you visit on a spring day you will find nearby Dora's Field (bought for, and named after, the poet's daughter) awash with wild daffodils. Even those who cannot recall another line of his poetry will know about the 'host of golden daffodils', though the genesis of the poem is a walk that his sister Dorothy took along the shores of Ullswater.

TROUTBECK   MAP REF NY4002

With its houses spread out along narrow country lanes, without any recognisable centre, Troutbeck would hardly seem to qualify as a village. The groupings are based around a number of wells and springs, which, until recent times, were the only source of drinking water in the area. However, lovers of vernacular architecture will find a superb collection of buildings, dating from the 16th to the 19th centuries, that retain original features such as mullioned windows, heavy cylindrical chimneys and a rare example of an exposed spinning gallery. Troutbeck is now designated a Conservation Area.

The best-preserved (if not the oldest) building in the Troutbeck valley is Townend, a fine example of a yeoman farmer's house. Townend offers a fascinating glimpse into what domestic life was like for Lakeland's wealthier farmers, with low ceilings, original home-carved oak panelling and furniture, and stone-flagged floors.

■ Visit

LAKELAND WILDLIFE OASIS

At Hale, south of Milnthorpe, working models, hands-on exhibits, computer programs and a range of live animals demonstrate the evolution of life on earth. There are free-flying butterflies, exotic vegetation, fish, reptiles, birds and mammals, plus a gift shop and a café.

■ Insight

THE NATIONAL PARK

The National Park Authority's main aims are to promote conservation, public enjoyment and the well-being of the local community. The biggest landowner within the Lake District National Park is the National Trust, which looks after large tracts of some of the finest Lakeland landscapes for the enjoyment of future generations. The Forestry Commission is another major landowner. United Utilities, too, owns three large areas within the National Park, which include Haweswater, Thirlmere and Ennerdale. Most of the land is, however, in the hands of individual farmers and estates.

ULVERSTON MAP REF SD2878

Ulverston, on the fringe of Morecambe Bay, is sufficiently off the beaten track to maintain an unhurried air, though Thursdays and Saturdays find the market square thronged with stalls. On top of Hoad Hill, overlooking the town, is a 90-foot (27.4m) copy of the Eddystone Lighthouse. It is no help to ships, however, being a monument to Sir John Barrow, Ulverston-born in 1764. A founder member of the Royal Geographical Society, his story is told in the town's heritage centre.

In Upper Brook Street the Laurel and Hardy Museum is a honeypot for those who can't hear the *Cuckoo Waltz* without thinking of the bowler-hatted buffoons of the silver screen. It is not so much a museum as a haphazard collection of Laurel and Hardy memorabilia, assembled here because Stan Laurel was born in Ulverston in 1890.

No souvenir is deemed too trivial for inclusion in the displays and visitors can watch clips from some of the pair's 105 films in a tiny cinema shoehorned into a corner of the museum.

WINDERMERE & BOWNESS-ON-WINDERMERE

MAP REF SD4198/4097

To many visitors, a visit to the Lakes implies nothing more strenuous than mooching around the shops of Windermere and Bowness, and a relaxing boat trip on the lake. It cannot be denied that these twin towns (almost joined into one these days) attract a disproportionate number of holiday-makers; those in search of the National Park's ethos, 'quiet recreation', should look elsewhere. Though traffic congestion is a perennial problem around the area, walkers can escape the crowds surprisingly quickly – even on the busiest of bank holidays.

The popularity of Windermere and Bowness is largely historical. Windermere is as far into the heart of the Lake District as the railway was ever driven. William Wordsworth lamented the coming of the railway; he foresaw that his beloved Lakeland would be spoiled irretrievably by an influx of visitors. Certainly the railway opened up the Lakeland landscape to working people, instead of just the well-heeled travellers with time on their hands. Wordsworth was right, of course – the Lake District has changed. On the other hand, millions of people are now able to enjoy the unrivalled scenery.

It may seem a bit odd that it is Windermere, rather than Bowness at the water's edge, that takes its name from the lake. This was to provide the railway station with a more appealing name; until the branch line opened in 1847, Windermere was known as Birthwaite.

Bowness offers the hordes of visitors a warm welcome, and is continually developing new enterprises for their pleasure. A few years ago it was hard to find a decent place to eat; now you can take your pick from a wide array of good places, including bistros, cafés, Indian restaurants, pizza parlours and the ever-popular fish and chip take-aways.

The water of England's longest lake laps gently on the beach at Bowness Bay. Swans and ducks, fed by visitors, enjoy an indolent lifestyle. Sleek clinker-built dinghies can be hired by the hour. The less energetic can enjoy a lake-long cruise, via Waterhead and Lakeside (linking to the steam trains of the restored Lakeside–Haverthwaite Railway), on the cruise ships *Tern*, *Teal* and *Swan*. *Tern*, with sleek lines and upturned prow, is more than a hundred years old and was once steam-powered. Since 2005, when the National Park Authority's hotly contested 10mph water speed limit took effect, Windermere has become a more peaceful lake.

Opposite Bowness Bay is Belle Isle. In 1774, when notions of the 'romantic' and 'picturesque' were at their height, a Mr English built an eccentric residence. Its round design brought so much ridicule on his head (Wordsworth called it 'a pepperpot') that Mr English was prompted to sell his unusual home.

Insight

ROMAN ROAD
The Troutbeck valley is one way that you can use to reach the spectacular Kirkstone Pass (the other route is via Ambleside). The valley was designated by the Romans to be starting point for a remarkable road, High Street, which took a – typically – uncompromising route straight across the mountain ridges that lie between the lakes of Ullswater and Haweswater.

The road is believed to have been built to link the Roman forts at Ambleside and Brougham with their port at Ravenglass on the west coast.

Activity

ULVERSTON'S CANAL
Ulverston has the shortest canal in Britain. It is just 1 mile (1.6km) long and links the town to the sea. Built by engineer John Rennie in 1794, it represents the high point of Ulverston's iron-ore industrial history; near by were the town's foundry and blast furnace. Ships could navigate along the canal into the town to be loaded with cargoes of iron and slate.

The canal had a short working life of just 50 years, after which it was rendered redundant by the railway. Ulverston also went into decline as the iron-ore industry gradually moved to Barrow.

Today the canal tow path (you can find the canal basin off Canal Street, on the A590) provides a pleasant walk down to the sea.

Visit

TRADITIONAL SPORTS
Traditional Lakeland sports are held at Ambleside on the Thursday before the first Monday in August. Events include fell racing, hound trails, and Cumberland and Westmorland wrestling.

The island site was earlier occupied by a manor house, which was besieged by troops of Roundheads while the Royalist owner was busy fighting in Carlisle. Archaeological finds reveal Belle Isle was occupied during Roman times. It was bought in 1781 as a present for Mrs Isabella Curwen, and renamed in the lady's honour. While most of Windermere's little islands are now owned by the National Trust, Belle Isle is still privately owned.

At the bottom of Bowness Hill, a couple of minutes' walk from the lake, is The Old Laundry, which caters for visitors and locals alike. As well as a theatre, there is a regular programme of exhibitions and events. Here, too, you'll find the World of Beatrix Potter, which uses the latest technology to bring to life the stories of Peter Rabbit, Jemima Puddleduck and many other characters.

Just a mile and a half (2.4km) from the centre of Bowness is a house of exquisite beauty. Completed in 1900 for the Manchester brewing mogul Sir Edward Holt, Blackwell was designed by Mackay Hugh Baillie Scott as an astounding expression of the Arts and Crafts Movement. Today it has been restored after decades of neglect and astonishingly almost all of the distinctive decorative features have remained intact. In room after room, now also furnished with authentic items from the period, you'll find delightful details and interplays of light, all with the majestic backdrop of lake and distant fell. The White Drawing Room is considered to be one of the finest interior designs of its period. Blackwell is also

an important exhibition space for ceramics, textiles, jewellery and furniture by contemporary artists.

A further 2.5 miles (4km) north along the Ambleside road brings you to Brockhole, a fine house in gardens that shelve down to the lake shore. Built for a Manchester businessman, the house has, since the late 1960s, been the National Park Visitor Centre. Brockhole is an excellent first stop for visitors new to the Lake District. There are gardens, displays, exhibitions, an adventure playground and a calendar of events.

The eastern shore of Windermere is, for much of its length, in private hands. Mill owners who prospered from the trade in wool and cotton eagerly bought up plots of land to create tranquil oases with views of the lake. Thus it is that the drive along the lake (on the A592) can be disappointing; there are few public access points to the water's edge. The less-populated western shore, much of it in the stewardship of the National Trust, however, offers lakeside walking.

For an elevated view of the lake, take a path to the left of the Windermere Hotel (at the top of the town). Within a few minutes you will be able to enjoy a glorious view of the lake and the southern Lakeland fells from the vantage point of Orrest Head. Another excellent viewpoint is the rounded hill called Gummer's How, which can be approached via a minor road just north of Newby Bridge. From the top (half an hour's walk from the car park) you will be able to see almost the length of Windermere, making the yachts and motor boats seem like tiny toys.

From Elterwater to Loughrigg Tarn

The little lake of Elter Water and petite Loughrigg Tarn are amongst the prettiest stretches of water in the lakeland, with bluebell woods, swans and a waterfall. Each season paints a different picture here, with golden daffodils by Langdale Beck in early spring, bluebells in Rob Rash woods in May, yellow maple in Elterwater village in October and a thousand shades of green, everywhere, all summer. This is very much a walk for all seasons and there are outstanding views throughout its length.

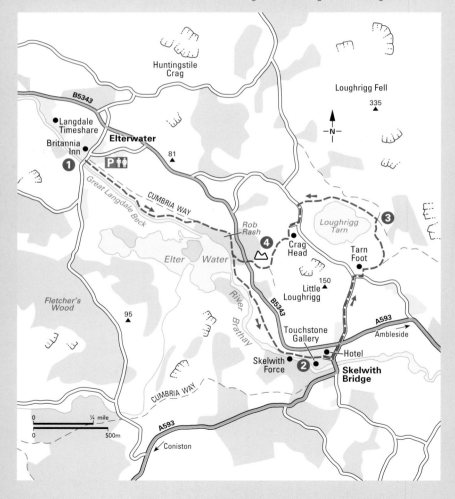

Route Directions

1 Pass through a small gate to walk downstream above Great Langdale Beck. Continue to enter the mixed woods of Rob Rash. A little gate leads through the stone wall; the open foot of Elter Water lies to the right. Continue along the path through the meadows above the river. Note that this section can be wet and is prone to flooding. Pass through the gate and enter mixed woods. Keep along the path to pass Skelwith Force waterfall down to the right. A little bridge leads across a channel to a viewing point above the falls. Keep along the path to pass through industrial buildings belonging to Kirkstone Quarry.

2 Touchstone Gallery is on the right, as the path becomes a small surfaced road. Continue to intercept the A593 by the bridge over the river where there are picnic benches. Turn left to pass the hotel. At the road junction, cross over the Great Langdale road to a lane that passes by the end of the cottages. Follow the lane, ascending to intercept another road. Turn right for a short distance and then left towards Tarn Foot farm. Bear right along the track, in front of the cottages. Where

the track splits, bear left. Through the gate carry on along the track to overlook Loughrigg Tarn. At a point half-way along the tarn cross the stile over the iron railings on the left.

3 Follow the footpath down the meadow to traverse right, just above the tarn. The footpath swings off right to climb a ladder stile over the stone wall. Follow the grassy track leading right, up the hill, to a gate and stile on to the road. Turn left along the road, until a surfaced drive leads up to the right, signed 'Public Footpath Skelwith Bridge'. Pass a small cottage and keep on the track to pass a higher cottage, Crag Head. A little way above this, a narrow grassy footpath leads off right, up the hillside, to gain a level shoulder between the craggy outcrops of Little Loughrigg.

4 Cross the shoulder and descend the path, passing a little tarnlet to the right, to intercept a stone wall. Keep left along the wall descending to find, in a few hundred paces, a ladder stile leading over the wall into the upper woods of Rob Rash. A steep descent leads down to the road. Cross this directly, and

go through the gap in the wall next to the large double gates. Descend a track to meet up with the outward route. Bear right to return to Elterwater village.

Route facts

DISTANCE/TIME 4 miles (6.4km) 2h

MAP OS Explorer OL7 The English Lakes (SE)

START National Trust pay-and-display car park, Elterwater; grid ref: NY 328048

TRACKS Grassy and stony paths and tracks, surfaced lane, 4 stiles

GETTING TO THE START Elterwater village lies about 5 miles (8km) west of Ambleside. At Skelwith Bridge turn on to the B5343 and soon bear left to reach the village. The main car park is on the left just before the bridge.

THE PUB Britannia Inn, Elterwater. Tel: 01539 437210; www.britinn.net

❶ Suitability: all ages

■ TOURIST INFORMATION CENTRES

Ambleside
Central Buildings,
Market Cross.
Tel: 01539 432582

Bowness-on-Windermere
Glebe Road, Bowness Bay.
Tel: 01539 442895

Brockhole, National Park Visitor Centre
On the A591, Windermere.
Tel: 01539 446601

Coniston
Main car park.
Tel: 01539 441802

Grange-over-Sands
Victoria Hall, Main Street.
Tel: 01539 534026

Kendal
Town Hall, Highgate.
Tel: 01539 797516

Ulverston
Coronation Hall,
County Square.
Tel: 01229 587120

Windermere
Victoria Street.
Tel: 01539 446499

■ PLACES OF INTEREST

Abbot Hall Art Gallery
Kirkland, Kendal.
Tel: 01539 722464

Abbot Hall Museum of Lakeland Life and Industry
Details as Art Gallery above.

The Lakes Discovery Museum @ the Armitt
Rydal Road, Ambleside.
Tel: 01539 431212

Beatrix Potter Gallery
Main Street, Hawkshead.
Tel: 01539 436355

Blackwell
Bowness. Tel: 01539 446139

Brantwood
Coniston. Tel: 01539 441396

Cartmel Priory
Cartmel, Grange-over-Sands.
Tel: 01539 536261. Free.

Dove Cottage
Grasmere. Tel: 01539 435544

Heron Corn Mill
Mill Lane, Beetham.
Tel: 01539 564271

Hill Top
Near Sawrey.
Tel: 01539 436269

Holker Hall and Gardens
Cark-in-Cartmel,
Grange-over-Sands.
Tel: 01539 558328

Kendal Museum of Natural History and Archaeology
Station Road, Kendal.
Tel: 01539 721374

Laurel and Hardy Museum
Brogden Street,
Ulverston.
Tel: 01229 582292

Levens Hall
Kendal. Tel: 01539 560321

Quaker Tapestry Exhibition Centre
New Road, Kendal.
Tel: 01539 722975

Ruskin Museum
The Institute, Coniston.
Tel: 01539 441164

Rydal Mount
Rydal. Tel: 01539 433002

Sizergh Castle
Sizergh, near Kendal.
Tel: 01539 560951

Stott Park Bobbin Mill
Near Newby Bridge.
Tel: 01539 531087

Swarthmoor Hall
Ulverston.
Tel: 01229 583204

Townend
Troutbeck, Windermere.
Tel: 01539 432628

The World of Beatrix Potter
The Old Laundry, Bowness-on-Windermere.
Tel: 01539 488444

■ FOR CHILDREN

The Aquarium of the Lakes
Lakeside, Newby Bridge.
Tel: 015395 30153

Lakeside and Haverthwaite Railway
Lakeside, Newby Bridge.
Tel: 01539 531594

■ SHOPPING

Ambleside
Market, Wed.

Kendal
Market, Wed & Sat.

Ulverston
Market, Thu & Sat.

LOCAL SPECIALITIES

Cumberland Sausage
Local butchers and markets.

Farmers' Markets
Kendal, Market Place, last Fri
of month.
Milnthorpe, second Sat of
month.

Ulverston, outside Market
Hall, third Sat of month.

Farm Shops

Low Sizergh Barn, Low
Sizergh Farm, Sizergh,
Kendal. Tel: 01539 560426
Sillfield Farm, Endmoor,
Kendal. Tel: 01539 567609

Gingerbread

The Gingerbread Shop,
Grasmere. Tel: 01539 435428

Hawkshead Relish

The Square, Hawkshead.
Tel: 01539 436614. Also from
many specialist food shops.

Herdwick Lamb

Local butchers and markets.

Morecambe Bay Shrimps

Available from local
fishmongers.

■ PERFORMING ARTS

The Brewery Arts Centre

Kendal. Tel: 01539 725133

Coronation Hall

Ulverston. Tel: 01229 588994

The Old Laundry Theatre

Crag Brow, Bowness-on-
Windermere.
Tel: 01539 488444.
Aug–Dec only.

■ OUTDOOR ACTIVITIES

BOAT TRIPS

Coniston

Coniston Launch,
Pier Cottage, Coniston.
Tel: 017687 75753
Steam Yacht *Gondola*,
Gondola Pier, Coniston.
Tel: 01539 441288

Windermere

Windermere Lake Cruises,
Lakeside, Newby Bridge,
Ulverston. Tel: 01539 443360

**COUNTRY PARKS, FORESTS
& NATURE RESERVES**

Grizedale Forest Park,
Grizedale. Tel: 01229 860010;
www.forestry.gov.uk

CYCLE HIRE

Ambleside

Biketreks, Rydal Road.
Tel: 01539 431245

Grizedale Forest

Grizedale Mountain Bikes,
Tel: 01229 860369; www.
grizedalemountainbikes.co.uk

Staveley

Millennium Cycles, Crook
Road. Tel: 01539 821167

Windermere

Country Lanes, Windermere
Railway Station.
Tel: 01539 444544

CYCLE ROUTES

The W2W, Walney to Wear
route through South Lakeland
to the Eden Valley and the
Pennines.
www.cyclingw2w.info

HORSE-RIDING

Kendal

Holmescales Riding Centre,
Holmescales Farm, Old
Hutton. Tel: 01539 729388

Windermere

Lakeland Pony Trekking,
Limefitt Park, Troutbeck,
Windermere.
Tel: 01539 431999; www.
lakelandponytrekking.co.uk

■ ANNUAL EVENTS & CUSTOMS

Ambleside

Rushbearing Ceremony,
first Sat in Jul.
Ambleside Sports, late Jul.
Lake District Summer Music
Festival, early to mid-Aug.

Cartmel

Cartmel Steeplechases,
Spring Bank Holiday.
Agricultural Show, early Aug.
Cartmel Races, Aug Band
Holiday.

Coniston

Coniston Water Festival,
early Jul.

Grange-over-Sands

Edwardian Festival, mid-Jun.
Lakeland Rose Show, Jul.

Grasmere

Sports and Show, end Aug.
Rushbearing Ceremony,
early Aug.

Kendal

Kendal Torchlight Procession,
early Sep.
Westmorland County Show,
early Sep.

Kirkby Lonsdale

Lunesdale Show, mid-Aug.
Country Fair, early Sep.

Rydal

Rydal Sheepdog Trials, Aug.

Staveley

Lake District Sheepdog
Trials, early Aug.

Ulverston

North Lonsdale Agricultural
Show, late Jul.
Lantern Procession, Sep.

Tea Rooms

The Apple Pie Eating House and Bakery
Rydal Road,
Ambleside LA22 9AN
Tel: 01539 433679

Lakeland gingerbread is just one of the favourites here. With views over Bridge House and the hills, it's the ideal spot to enjoy the delicious treats, baked dishes or just a cappuccino.

Hat Trick Café
Yew Tree Barn,
Low Newton LA11 6JP
Tel: 01539 530577

The A590 no longer rumbles through this South Lakeland hamlet, but you should make a diversion on your way to Newby Bridge to stop off for breakfast, a light lunch, or perhaps afternoon tea with warm chocolate fudge cake and a glass of their home-made lemonade.

Hazlemere Café and Bakery
1 Yewbarrow Terrace,
Grange-over-Sands
LA11 6ED
Tel: 01539 532972

Taste more than 25 different types of cuppa at this traditional Victorian tea room. Local specialities include Cumberland Rum Nicky and pheasant burgers.

Low Sizergh Barn Farm Shop and Tearoom
Kendal LA8 8AE
Tel: 01539 560426
www.lowsizerghbarn.co.uk

Using the freshest local ingredients from its farm shop, this is a popular stop.

Jumble Room
Langdale Road,
Grasmere LA22 9SU
Tel: 01539 435188
www.thejumbleroom.co.uk

A café/restaurant, the Jumble Room creates tempting dishes from 'Thailand to Troutbeck'.

Pubs

Drunken Duck
Barngates,
Ambleside LA22 0NG
Tel: 01539 436347
www.drunkenduckinn.co.uk

This pub is popular with walkers and cyclists taking in the excellent beer and food, and the fine views.

Golden Rule
Smithy Brow, Ambleside
LA22 9AS
Tel: 01539 432257

Considered by many to be one of the few true pubs, this is a haven of good crack in front of real log fires. Beers are from Robinsons, and the food is limited, but the welcome is warm.

Old Dungeon Ghyll Hotel
Great Langdale,
Ambleside LA22 9JY
Tel: 01539 437272
www.odg.co.uk

The ODG's often full to overflowing with walkers, climbers and campers. Its reputation rests on its excellent beer and good value food. The enviable setting, below the towering Langdale Pikes, probably helps.

Mason's Arms
Strawberry Bank, Cartmel
Fell LA11 6NW. Tel: 01539
568486; www.masonsarms
strawberrybank.co.uk

Situated on a bend in a minor road as it climbs Strawberry Bank, the Mason's Arms is a popular stop on the scenic back road to Newby Bridge. There are great views from the terrace over the Winster Valley, and the interior includes a large dining area.

Black Bull
1 Yewdale Road,
Coniston LA21 8DU
Tel: 01539 441335
www.conistonbrewery.com

Built around 400 years ago, this spacious old coaching inn is well supplied by the excellent brewery to its rear. Bar meals are pretty standard, but the restaurant offers superb dishes.

Eskdale & Wasdale

The southern peninsulas of Cartmel and Furness attract fewer visitors but still have plenty to offer. The delightful narrow-gauge Ravenglass and Eskdale Railway, which once transported iron-ore from the Eskdale mines to the coast, now steams along the valleys of the rivers Esk and Mite carrying tourists and hikers alike, while unspoiled Dunnerdale is a haven for those in search of solitude amid delightful scenery. The superb coastal area offers much to walkers, birders and lovers of quiet places.

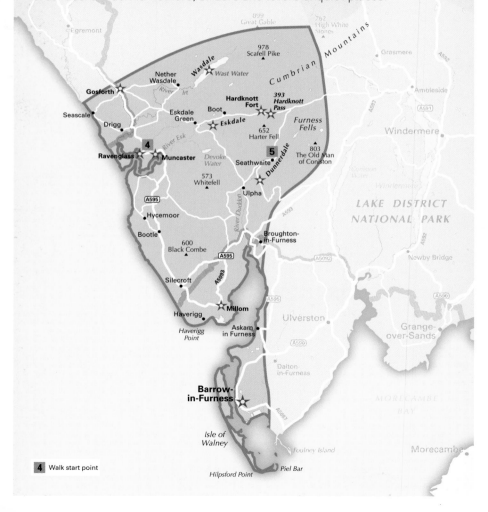

4 Walk start point

HOT SPOTS

Unmissable attractions

In this area you will find England's highest mountain, Scafell Pike, its deepest lake, Wast Water and plenty of opportunities for fantastic walks and cycle rides. Don't pass through Nether Wasdale without lingering among its woodlands. Delightful paths through the tranquil oak woods lead to the shores of Wast Water, where you can look across to expansive steel-cold screes that fan out from murky and mysterious gullies in Whin Rigg's rockfaces. This is a fragile environment, where purple saxifrage and alpine lady's mantle grows in the gullies and peregrine falcons nest on the cliff edges and precipitous crags around Buckbarrow.

1

1 Eskdale
These peaceful hills were once a Norman hunting preserve. This is excellent walking country, with plentiful rights of way and room to roam.

2 Wast Water
From the Wasdale Head road you get a grand view over Wast Water towards the slopes of Yewbarow and Great Gable. While you're there, be sure to seek out Wasdale Head church. One of the smallest churches in the country, it is almost lost within a tiny copse of trees.

3 Muncaster Castle
Blessed with superb views, parts of Muncaster Castle date back to medieval times. The majority of the building is however, the result of the extensive reconstruction which took place in 1862.

4 Hardknott Roman fort
Situated at the western end of Hardknott Pass, this Roman fort was built in the 2nd century AD and commands an isolated position overlooking Eskdale. The walled and ramparted fort covered about 3 acres (1.2ha) and the ruins include fragments of watchtowers and a bath house.

BARROW-IN-FURNESS

MAP REF SD2068

Even the most loyal of locals would hesitate to describe Barrow as beautiful. Until the mid-19th century there was just a tiny fishing village here, on the tip of the Furness peninsula. What made it grow at an astonishing rate were the iron- and steel-making industries, closely followed, logically, by the construction of ships.

The shipbuilding company of Vickers became almost synonymous with Barrow, and even today, long after the great days of British shipbuilding have gone, the docks and shipyards are an impressive sight. For a fascinating overview of the industry, past and present, head for one of the town's most popular attractions, the Dock Museum on North Road. Sitting astride a deep dry dock, the museum tells how, in the space of a generation, Barrow became a major force in maritime engineering. Other museum exhibits focus on older shipbuilding traditions, and the pioneers whose foresight and inventiveness helped Britain to lead the way.

A surprise awaits those visitors who drive past the museum – a road bridge links Barrow with the Isle of Walney. A cursory glance at the map shows this to be a geographic oddity shielding the tip of the Furness peninsula, and Barrow itself, from the ravages of the sea. The southern tip of the Isle of Walney is a haven for wildlife.

Between Barrow and Dalton, in the 'Vale of Deadly Nightshade', is Furness Abbey. Now an evocative ruin of weathered, salmon-coloured sandstone, it was, in its heyday, second in importance only to Fountains Abbey in North Yorkshire. Separated from the rest of England by sea and mountains, Furness Abbey achieved a remarkable degree of feudal independence, owning outlying farms, known as granges, as far afield as Lincolnshire and Ireland. Parts of the abbey (now in the hands of English Heritage) still stand to substantially their full height, in a romantic wooded setting. The towers, arches and windows rise up in an architectural embodiment of Christian faith; the size of the community can be estimated by the fact that the monks' dormitory is 200 feet (61m) long.

The nearby village of Dalton-in-Furness, just a quiet backwater, was once the capital of Furness and the main market town for the area; but that role has passed now to Ulverston and Barrow. On one side of the old market square is Dalton Castle, an uncompromisingly square sandstone building that was built by the monks of Furness Abbey as a courthouse and prison. It was restored in the 1960s, after the Castle was obtained by the National Trust from the Duke of Buccleuch.

■ Insight

FURNESS PENINSULA

The young William Wordsworth made a number of trips, on horseback, to the Furness peninsula. The red sandstone ruins of Furness Abbey inspired him to feature them in The Prelude and a couple of sonnets. He knew Barrow-in-Furness too, but only as a small village as yet untouched by the shipbuilding industry that transformed the town so rapidly.

Over Muncaster Fell

Muncaster Fell is a long and knobbly fell of no great height. A winding path negotiates the fell from end to end and this lovely linear walk takes you from Ravenglass to Eskdale Green, returning on 'Laal Ratty', a narrow-gauge train.

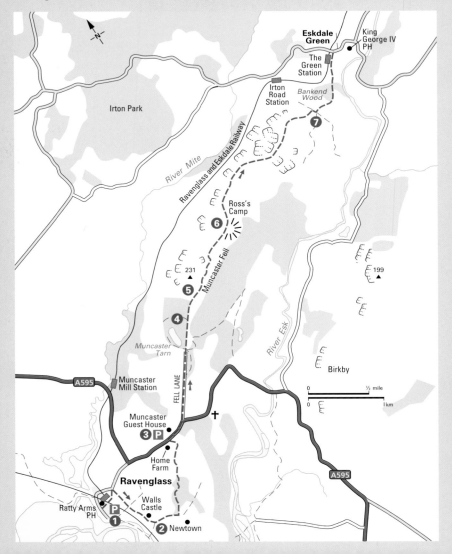

Route Directions

1 Leave the car park by crossing the mainline and miniature railway line, using the footbridges, then follow a narrow path to a road junction. Turn right on a footpath by the side of a narrow road, signposted 'Walls Castle'. The bath house is soon on the left.

2 Continue along the access road and turn left along a track signposted 'Newtown'. Turn left again before the cottage and follow another track up a little wooded valley. Go through four gates, following the track from the wood, across fields and into another wood. Turn left to reach Home Farm and a busy main road.

3 Cross the road and turn right, passing Muncaster Castle car park and the Muncaster Guest House. The road leads up to a bend, where Fell Lane is signposted uphill. Ascend the clear track, cross a little wooded dip, then fork right and left, noticing Muncaster Tarn on the left. Go through a gate at the top of the lane to reach Muncaster Fell.

4 A path forges through boggy patches along the edge of a coniferous plantation, then the path runs free across the slopes of Muncaster Fell. A path rising to the left leads to the summit, otherwise keep right to continue.

5 Views develop as the path winds about on the slope overlooking Eskdale. A panorama of fells opens up as a curious structure is reached at Ross's Camp. Here, a large stone slab was turned into a picnic table for a shooting party in 1883.

6 Continue along the footpath, looping round a broad and boggy area to reach a corner of a dry-stone wall. Go down through a gateway and bear in mind that the path can be muddy. There is a short ascent on a well-buttressed stretch, then the descent continues on a sparsely wooded slope, through a gate, ending on a track near another gate.

7 Go through the gate and then turn left, crossing a field to reach a stone wall seen at the edge of Bankend Wood. Walk on keeping to the right side of the wall to reach a stile and a stream. A narrow track continues, becoming better as it draws close to a road. Turn left at the end of the road to reach The Green Station.

Route facts

DISTANCE/TIME
6 miles (9.7km) 2h30

MAP OS Explorer OL6
The English Lakes (SW)

START Car park at Ravenglass, close to station; grid ref: SD 085964

FINISH Eskdale Green Station; grid ref: SD 145998

TRACKS Clear tracks and paths, muddy after rain, 1 stile

GETTING TO THE START
Ravenglass is right on the coast, south of Seascale, accessed via a turn-off from the A595. Follow this road down into the village and the signed car park.

THE PUB King George IV Inn, Eskdale Green, near the end of the route.
Tel: 01946 723262;
www.kinggeorge-eskdale.co.uk

❶ Moderately rough descents and wet ground likely. Suitability: children 8+

DUNNERDALE MAP REF SD2195

Dunnerdale is as delightful and unspoiled as it was when William Wordsworth first explored the valley. The River Duddon rises in the hills by the Wrynose Pass, and reaches the sea at its own estuary of Duddon Sands. In between are 10 miles (16km) of the most delectable scenery – not the most dramatic, nor the most spectacular, but those who love more intimate landscapes will find Dunnerdale a delight.

The handsome little town of Broughton-in-Furness stands back from the Duddon estuary. The market square, dominated by a huge chestnut tree, boasts a stepped obelisk and a pair of stone tables that were once used to sell fish caught in the River Duddon.

From Duddon Bridge a minor road takes you up Dunnerdale. You are seldom far from the river, which is rocky and fast flowing, and the natural habitat of dippers and wagtails. There are grassy riverbanks that seem designed for spreading out a picnic blanket. Ulpha, a straggle of houses and farmsteads, is the only village of any size in the valley.

■ Visit

THE SWINSIDE STONE CIRCLE

The Swinside Stone Circle can be found on a spur of Black Combe, a little-explored fell, off the A596 between Millom and Broughton-in-Furness. Though lying on private land, the circle of 57 standing stones can be viewed from an adjacent right of way. The circle is similar in size to Castlerigg stone circle, near Keswick, though its setting is somewhat bleaker.

As you continue to climb, the fields and woods give way to a more rugged landscape, as Harter Fell at 2,139 feet (652m) and the higher peaks of central Lakeland begin to dominate the view. When you reach a road junction, at Cockley Beck, your choice is between two of the most spectacular routes in the country, you can either travel west to Eskdale via the tortuous Hardknott Pass, or east, along Wrynose Pass, and down into the beautiful Little Langdale valley.

ESKDALE MAP REF NY1701

Here is another beautiful valley that remains relatively quiet when so many other places are busy with tourists. The reason is inaccessibility; to explore Eskdale most people will have to negotiate the twists, turns and hairpin bends of the Hardknott and Wrynose passes, or else take the long way round, meandering through south Lakeland. All the better, then, for those who venture this far west, for Eskdale is well worth the effort.

This is excellent walking country, with plentiful rights of way and room to roam. For more than 30 years the Ravenglass and Eskdale Railway has enabled hikers and sightseers to venture into the heart of Eskdale without blocking up the narrow road with their cars. This delightful narrow-gauge railway used to carry iron ore from the Eskdale mines to the coast; now the engines carry passengers up the valley. There are seven stations along the line, all offering opportunities for scenic walks with the option of taking a later train back down to Ravenglass.

The terminus, at Dalegarth, is just a short walk from Boot, a tiny village with a friendly pub, the Boot Inn. Just up the valley, the Woolpack recalls a time when this was a watering hole for the men who drove packponies heavily laden with fleeces down to the coast. Beyond a packhorse bridge spanning Whillan Beck is the delectable grouping of tiny buildings that comprise Eskdale Mill. Cereals have been ground here since 1578, but milling ended during the 1920s. The overshot waterwheel was adapted to supply electricity to upper Eskdale; the valley was connected to the mains in 1955.

GOSFORTH MAP REF NY0603

Sandwiched between Wasdale and Sellafield – 'beauty and the beast', you could say – is the village of Gosforth. Vikings, settling in the area, were gradually converted to the Christian faith, and the sandstone church at Gosforth boasts a number of artefacts dating back to this period, more than 1,000 years ago. In the churchyard is a Viking cross that is 14 feet (4.3m) high and so slender that the wonder is that it has survived intact. Intricate carving on all four sides combines Viking legends with Christian teaching.

Another ancient cross in the churchyard was converted, in a fit of official vandalism two centuries ago, into a sundial. Other relics, now displayed inside the church, fared better: the Fishing Stone and a pair of hogback tombstones are potent symbols of the coming together, many centuries ago, of two disparate cultures.

■ Activity

W2W CYCLE ROUTE

The Walney to Wear Cycle Route was inspired by the success of the Coast to Coast route, which runs from St Bees. The W2W, Sustrans regional route 20, crosses the Lake District peninsulas in easy stages to Kendal before heading up the Lune Gorge, then across the Eden Valley and over the Pennines. Its total route is 151 miles (241km) from Walney Island to Wearmouth, near Sunderland.

HARDKNOTT PASS & ROMAN FORT MAP REF NY2301

When you gaze down from the remains of the fort at the western end of the Hardknott Pass (1,291 feet/393m) it is easy to see why the Romans chose this site. Hardknott Castle Roman Fort (owned by English Heritage) enjoys a commanding position down into the green valley of Eskdale. Attacks from three sides were impossible and a trench forestalled attacks from the east.

Soldiers were garrisoned here to safeguard the road they had constructed to link the fort at Ambleside and the port of Ravenglass. Preferring to take the most direct route, they drove their road over the most difficult terrain through the Hardknott and Wrynose passes.

Despite the wonderful views, the Roman soldiers must have regarded isolated, windswept Mediobogdum as an unglamorous posting. The perimeter wall is of typical playing-card shape and the ruins are still impressive. The soldiers drilled on a flat parade ground near by. The bath house would have been one of their few comforts.

Hardknott Pass, rising 1,000 feet (305m) out of Eskdale in little more than a mile (1.6km), is one of the most spectacular roads in the country; a few of the hairpin bends are as steep as 1-in-3 (33%). The ascent holds fewer terrors for car drivers these days; most problems arise at peak holiday times. But if the road is icy, or you are towing a caravan, don't even consider it!

MILLOM MAP REF SD1780

Sitting on its own peninsula overlooking the estuary of the River Duddon, Millom is well off the beaten track. The town grew with the iron and steel industries in the latter years of the 19th century. The Millom Folk Museum and the Tourist Information Centre are both housed in the imaginatively redeveloped railway station. The museum has vivid reminders of the town's iron-mining days, including an impressive full-scale reconstruction of an iron-ore drift mine, as well as items associated with Norman Nicholson, Millom's own poet.

The Hodbarrow Iron Works, which closed in the 1960s, have been encouraged to go back to nature. The result is a brackish lagoon, adjacent to the Duddon Estuary, which is now an RSPB reserve. This stretch of water acts as a magnet for breeding wildfowl, waders and the rare natterjack toad.

MUNCASTER CASTLE

MAP REF SD1096

Few stately homes can boast a view to match the panorama from the terrace of Muncaster Castle. Directly below are gardens, featuring one of the largest collection of rhododendrons in the country. In the middle distance the River Esk meanders prettily through the lowlands. The horizon is taken up by a frieze of starkly delineated Lakeland peaks, of which Scafell Pike at 3,210 feet (978m) is the most prominent.

In 1208 the land at Muncaster was granted to the Pennington family, and is still in the family's ownership today. The sandstone castle is a major addition to a 14th-century pele tower. Visitors get a guided tour (on audio tape, at least) by the present owner, detailing the many treasures and artworks to be found.

Muncaster Castle is also the headquarters of the World Owl Trust, which is dedicated to worldwide owl conservation. Visitors can see a variety of owls, from the pygmy owl to the gigantic eagle owl, and from our own native species to some of the rarest owls in the world. On fine summer afternoons visitors get a chance to meet the birds and, weather permitting, watch them in flight.

As Lords of the Manor, the Pennington family owned Muncaster Mill from the 15th century right up to 1961, when the mill closed. The present buildings, dating from about 1700, are easily reached by car on the A595 or by taking a ride on the Ravenglass and Eskdale Railway (the mill is a request halt on the line). The tiny mill, with its overshot wheel turned by water from the River Mite, is a reminder of a time when every village had its own corn mill. Though now restored to full working order, the mill is currently closed and its future is again uncertain.

Seathwaite and the Duddon Valley

William Wordsworth loved the Duddon Valley so much that he wrote many sonnets about it. Follow in his footsteps by a chattering beck and through a gorge, where little has changed since his day. There's tarmac on those winding, walled lanes, but the byres and woods and lively stream are still untouched.

Route Directions

1 From the Newfield Inn at Seathwaite in Dunnerdale follow the main valley road past the little church, then turn right on the tarmac lane towards Turner Hall Farm. Leave this and follow a track on the left through a gate marked 'High Moss'. Where the track ends, keep to the left-hand side of the farm,

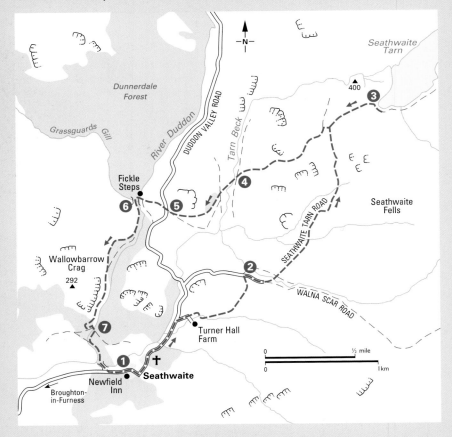

go through the top gate and follow the field path out to the Walna Scar Road.

2 Turn right along the road, then left on to the utility company's access road to Seathwaite Tarn. This pleasant track climbs steadily to the reservoir dam.

3 Retrace your steps for around 200 paces to a waymarking post highlighting a downhill path that weaves through rock and rough pasture. Crossing over a tiny beck it continues down to a gate, leading to a boggy field. On the far side of this, another gate leads to a ladder stile on the right.

4 Cross the stile and footbridge over Tarn Beck. On the opposite bank turn left and follow an obvious, wet, path through a gate and on along the edge of a wood. Pass behind a lovely cottage and continue in the wood past a barn on the left until the path rises to enter open country. Continue on this marshy way to the road.

5 Across the road follow the signed bridleway to the Fickle Steps, huge boulders, which allow you to cross the River Duddon. (Caution: if the river is in spate here and the steps are underwater, return by the road.)

6 To continue on the route, turn left, go over the footbridge across Grassguards Gill, then climb along a waymarked path above the tight wooded Wallowbarrow Gorge. The footpath descends again to cross boulder-strewn terrain on the bank of the River Duddon.

7 When you reach a tall one-arched footbridge, cross over to the other side of the river and turn right along the path, now tracing the eastern bank of the Duddon. Go over the footbridge spanning a tributary, Tarn Beck, before following a path out to the road. Turn left to walk back to your car in Seathwaite village.

Route facts

DISTANCE/TIME 5 miles (8km) 3h

MAP OS Explorer OL6 The English Lakes (SW)

START Seathwaite: roadside pull-off; grid ref: SD 231975, limited roadside parking near pub and church; grid ref: SD 228960

TRACKS Paths, tracks, can be muddy below Seathwaite Tarn, 9 stiles

GETTING TO THE START Seathwaite is on a minor road, 3 miles (4.8km) north of Ulpha and south of the Hardknott Pass. There are a few roadside parking spaces before the village (do not use those directly outside the pub), and a small lay-by opposite the church. If all these are full, continue for almost 1 mile (1.6km) to larger grassy spaces where the road meets open fellside (Point 5 on the walk).

THE PUB Newfield Inn, Seathwaite, Point 1 on route. Tel: 01229 716208; www.newfieldinn.co.uk

❶ River crossing by stepping stones, too far apart for younger children; also rough slopes above river. If river is low it may be possible for children to paddle, otherwise return to Seathwaite along road. Suitability: children 11+

RAVENGLASS MAP REF SD0896

The Roman fort and harbour of Ravenglass were known to the Romans as Glannoventa; up to 1,000 men were garrisoned here. Little remains of this settlement, just a short stroll to the south of the village, except for the ruins of the bath house. Rising to 12 feet (3.7m), these are probably the highest extant Roman ruins in the country.

Ravenglass today comprises a short street of houses that ends abruptly at a slipway down to the beach and the estuaries of the rivers Mite and Esk. Inaccessibility to everything but small craft, due to sandbars, meant that Ravenglass never developed as a port.

Nowadays, Ravenglass is synonymous with the Ravenglass and Eskdale Railway, affectionately known as 'Laal Ratty'. Though it is now one of the most popular visitor attractions in western Lakeland, the line has had a distinctly chequered career. The railway (with a 3-foot gauge track) was built in 1875, to carry iron ore (and a few passengers) from the Eskdale mines down to the coast and the main Furness line. When the mines became unprofitable, the railway closed.

Operating on a narrower 15-inch gauge track, the line reopened in 1913 to serve Eskdale's granite quarries and carry a few tourists. Trains plied the narrow-gauge track until they came to a halt once again, in 1953. Fortunately, a group of enthusiasts came to the rescue, helping to buy up the line in 1960, and running it as a tourist attraction. Today the miniature steam locos and carriages operate an extensive service over the seven highly scenic miles (11.2km) between Ravenglass and the terminus at Dalegarth.

WASDALE & WAST WATER

MAP REF NY1606

The bleakly beautiful valley of Wasdale must be approached from the west, and for most visitors that necessitates a lengthy drive. The reward is that Wasdale will be spectacularly empty at times when the Lakeland honeypots are straining under the weight of visitors. If the view up to the head of the valley seems oddly familiar, that's because the National Park Authority created their logo from this view of Wast Water and the three peaks – Yewbarrow, Great Gable and Lingmell – whose symmetry frames the view. Scafell Pike, near the head of the valley is, at 3,210 feet (978m), the highest peak in England.

Although it is just 3 miles (4.8km) long, Wast Water is the deepest lake in England. The huge screes that dominate the southern shore continue their descent fully 250 feet (76m) into the cool clear waters. Those who tire of the busy Windermere waters will relish the tranquillity and awesome landscape to be found at Wasdale.

The road hugs the water's edge until you reach Wasdale Head; communities don't come much smaller or more welcoming than this. The Wasdale Head Hotel is where walkers and climbers congregate to drink beer, take in some essential calories and swap tales of the mountains. Once you are ensconced in a comfortable chair it is easy to forget that you are miles from anywhere...

■ TOURIST INFORMATION CENTRES

Barrow-in-Furness
Forum 28, Duke Street.
Tel: 01229 876505

■ PLACES OF INTEREST

Dock Museum
North Road,
Barrow-in-Furness.
Tel: 01229 876400.
Free.

Eskdale Mill
Boot. Tel: 01946 723335

Furness Abbey
Barrow-in-Furness.
Tel: 01229 823420.
Extensive remains of the
Cistercian abbey built in 1147.

Hardknott Roman Fort
Hardknott Pass.
Remains of the Roman fort
can be seen at the western
end of Hardknott Pass.
Free.

Millom Folk Museum
Station Buildings,
Millom.
Tel: 01229 772555.
Room sets include a miner's
cottage and a blacksmith's
forge.

**Muncaster Castle,
Gardens and Owl Centre**
Muncaster.
Tel: 01229 717614
Headquarters of the World
Owl Trust.

**Ravenglass and
Eskdale Railway**
Ravenglass.
Tel: 01229 717171
Steam and diesel trains
run along a 7-mile (11.2km)
track, through beautiful
countryside, from Ravenglass
to Dalegarth.

**Ravenglass Roman
Bath House**
Ravenglass. Free.

■ FOR CHILDREN

**South Lakes
Wild Animal Park**
Broughton Road,
Dalton-in-Furness.
Tel: 01229 466086

■ SHOPPING

Barrow-in-Furness
Market, Wed, Fri & Sat.

Broughton-in-Furness
Market, Tue.

LOCAL SPECIALITIES

Crafts
The *Made in Cumbria* guide to
workshops and galleries is
available from Tourist
Information Centres. Their
website lists over 400
members (craftspeople and
artists) who produce
everything from gifts to
furniture and speciality foods,
all made in Cumbria.
www.madeincumbria.co.uk

Cumberland Sausage
Award-winning sausages and
hams at Woodall's of
Waberthwaite.
Tel: 01229 717237;
www.richardwoodall.co.uk

Cumberland Rum Butter
Available from many local
food shops.

Pottery
Gosforth Pottery, near
Seascale, Gosforth.
Tel: 01946 725296

■ PERFORMING ARTS

**Forum 28 Theatre
and Arts Centre**
28 Duke Street,
Barrow-in-Furness.
Tel: 01229 820000

■ OUTDOOR ACTIVITIES

SEA FISHING
There is good sea fishing
from the shoreline around the
Isle of Walney and Piel Island.
Sea fishing trips can be
arranged by Mr S McCoy.
Tel: 01229 826160

BEACH
Silecroft and Haverigg are
both award-winning,
extensive sandy beaches and
are likely to appeal to those
look for peace and solitude.

CYCLING

The Eskdale Trail

The Ravenglass and Eskdale Railway provides a virtually traffic-free route in this beautiful valley. Details from stations at Ravenglass or Dalegarth.

Wear to Wear (W2W) Cycle Route

This superb trans-Pennine route (Sustrans Regional Route 20) begins on Walney Island and traverses the southern lakes on its 151-mile (243km) path northeast.

GOLF COURSES

Askam-in-Furness

Dunnerholme Golf Club, Duddon Road.
Tel: 01229 462675

Barrow-in-Furness

Barrow Golf Club, Rakesmoor Lane, Hawcoat.
Tel: 01229 825444
Furness Golf Club, Central Drive, Isle of Walney.
Tel: 01229 471232

Silecroft

Silecroft Golf Club.
Tel: 01229 774250

GOLF DRIVING RANGE

Barrow-in-Furness

Furness Golf Centre, Hawthwaite Lane, near Roanhead.
Tel: 01229 465870

LONG-DISTANCE FOOTPATHS & TRAILS

The Cistercian Way

A 33-mile (52.8km) walk from Grange-over-Sands to Roa Island, near Barrow-in-Furness.

The Cumberland Way

An 82-mile (131.2km) crossing of the Lake District from Ravenglass to Appleby.

The Cumbria Coastal Way

A 124-mile (198.4km) walk from Silverdale to Carlisle.

The Furness Way

A 71-mile (114km) walk from Arnside to Ravenglass crossing the Furness Peninsula.

NATURE RESERVES

Haverigg Nature Reserve, near Millom.
North and South Walney Nature Reserves, Barrow-in-Furness.
Sandscales Haws, Barrow-in-Furness.

RUGBY

Barrow-in-Furness

Barrow Raiders Rugby League Football Club, Craven Park.
Tel: 01229 830470

■ ANNUAL EVENTS & CUSTOMS

Gosforth

Cumbria Riding Club Dressage Show, early Apr.
Gosforth Show, mid-Aug.
Cumbria Riding Club Hunter Trials, early Oct.

Millom

Millom and Broughton Show, West Park, Broughton-in-Furness, end Aug.

Muncaster

Muncaster Country Fair, Muncaster Castle, end Aug.

Wasdale

Wasdale Shepherd's Meet and Show, Wasdale Head, mid-Oct.

Tea Rooms

Fellbites

Dalegarth Station,
Boot, Eskdale CA19 1TF
Tel: 01229 717171
www.ravenglass-railway.co.uk
At the valley terminus of 'Laal Ratty' the Fellbites café can serve a trainload of passengers at a time with freshly cooked food using locally sourced ingredients wherever possible. And you're handy for the train back to Ravenglass!

Broughton Village Bakery

Princes Street,
Broughton-in-Furness
LA20 6HQ
Tel: 01229 716284
Using organic, Fairtrade beans, ground fresh to maximise their flavour, this is a splendid little retreat to enjoy a tall latte or a snappy espresso. You can get a light lunch or snack or try the tempting home-baked cakes.

The Square Café

Annan House, The Square,
Broughton-in-Furness
LA20 6JA
Tel: 01229 716388
www.thesquarecafe.biz
Overlooking the village square, with a few outside tables, this traditional café is popular with walkers, cyclists and motorcyclists. Afternoon teas with home-made scones are a favourite.

Woodlands

Santon Bridge, Near
Holmrook CA19 1UY
Tel: 01946 726281
www.santonbridge.co.uk
With a great view of the local red squirrels, Woodlands is attached to the Santon Bridge Craft Shop and concentrates on home-made food. Handy for Muncaster Castle and Eskdale as well as Wasdale.

Pubs

Boot Inn

Boot, Eskdale CA19 1TG
Tel: 01946 723224
www.bootinn.co.uk
Formerly known as the Burnmoor, this friendly pub is good for families. The new conservatory dining area boasts enviable views of the surrounding fells and the garden in the summer.

Newfield Inn

Seathwaite, Duddon Valley,
Broughton-in-Furness
LA20 6ED
Tel: 01229 716208
www.newfieldinn.co.uk
Deep in the remote Duddon Valley, the Newfield Inn is exactly how you would like to find it – stone floors, real fires, big oak beams. There's a good specials board for food, including pastas and fish, but the local Cumberland sausage is always a favourite.

King George IV Inn

Eskdale, Holmrook
CA19 1TS
Tel: 01946 723262
www.kinggeorge-eskdale.co.uk
This 17th-century coaching inn lies in one of Lakeland's finest hidden valleys. Inside you'll find open fires and flagged floors. You can try ostrich fillet or salmon in martini, orange and ginger at this venerable staging post at the junction near Eskdale Green station. Down to earth offerings include pizzas and steak in Old Peculiar pie, with a good range of beers.

The Bower House

Eskdale, Holmrook
CA19 1TD
Tel: 01946 723244
www.bowerhouseinn.co.uk
Children will love the outdoor play area. Adults may prefer the real ales and imaginative dishes, which use fresh local ingredients whenever possible. Look out for local Herdwick lamb with minted apple chutney, or the roasted haunch of venison with red wine and juniper berries.

Western Lakes

SCOTLAND

The western lakes and shores of Cumbria tell a different story from other parts of Lakeland. Their features rival the most beautiful in the area – idyllic Buttermere and imposing Great Gable – but this is also an industrial landscape, where men have hewn coal, slate and iron ore from the hills.

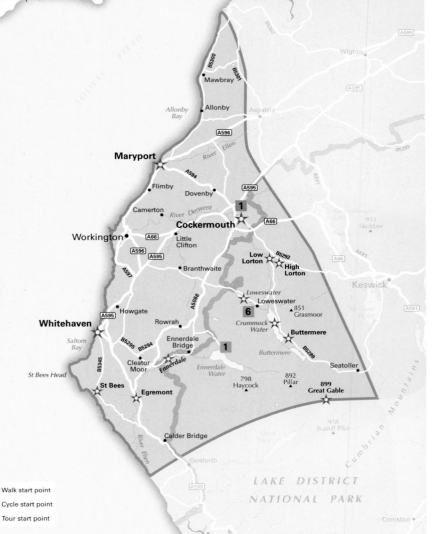

6 Walk start point

1 Cycle start point

1 Tour start point

LOWESWATER

Unmissable attractions

The western lakes and shores have features that rival the most beautiful areas, as well as an industrial history of mining coal, slate and iron ore. Lorton Vale sweeps south from the small market town of Cockermouth and the delightful Buttermere before ending in the lofty Honister Pass. Whitehaven was the third-largest port in Britain, thanks to local industries. Today it has a small fishing fleet, and the harbour has been declared a conservation area. St Bees is the start of Wainwright's famous 190-mile (304km) Coast-to-Coast walk to Robin Hood's Bay in North Yorkshire. This part of the Cumbrian coast is its only Heritage Coast, and part of the cliffs form St Bees Head Nature Reserve.

1

1 Buttermere
Surrounded by high hills, the gentle, 5-mile (8km), two-hour walk around the edge of Buttermere offers superb views throughout.

2 Ennerdale
This long, remote valley is fringed by high fells accessible only on foot. In the early years of the 21st century it was chosen for a groundbreaking 're-wilding' programme, following the felling of a large tract of commercial coniferous forest. Now the countryside is left to take its own course, without farmers or foresters intervening.

3 Napes Needle, Great Gable
W P Haskett Smith's remarkable ascent of the south face of Great Gable and Napes Needle, in June 1886, marked the beginning of English rock climbing as a sport. This route to the summit and Napes Needles is only for very experienced rock climbers but there are many less challenging routes up Great Gable suitable for fit walkers.

BUTTERMERE & CRUMMOCK WATER

MAP REF NY1716/NY1519

These two neighbouring lakes in the Buttermere valley, separated only by a half-mile (0.8km) strip of meadowland, were probably one lake originally. Buttermere is perhaps the more beautiful, although Crummock Water is twice its size and claims one of the most impressive waterfalls in the Lakes. Scale Force, on its western side, plunges 172 feet (52m) on its way to the lake. The path to Scale Force, however, begins in tiny Buttermere village, and is a rough walk to the tree-lined gorge through which Scale Beck plummets.

A path leads all the way along Crummock Water's western shore, to join up with the B5289, which runs down the eastern shore. This road links Lorton Vale to the north of Buttermere, with the steep Honister Pass to the east, and continues on to Borrowdale.

Buttermere is also surrounded by high hills, such as the 2,126-foot (648m) Fleetwith Pike which guards the Honister Pass and the 1,959-foot (597m) Hay Stacks. The easy two-hour walk around Buttermere is an impressive one, with superb views in all directions. To the northwest are the Derwent Fells, crossed only by the Newlands and Whinlatter passes, while to the west above Burtness Wood stands another range of dramatic crags and fells.

COCKERMOUTH   MAP REF NY1230

For a small country market town, Cockermouth has plenty of history behind it. The most significant event as far as most of today's visitors are concerned is that William Wordsworth was born here in 1770. If you first visit modest Dove Cottage in Grasmere, where the poet later lived, the grandeur of his birthplace, a Georgian town house dating from 1745, comes as a surprise. Wordsworth House has been faithfully restored by the National Trust and has been furnished in mid-18th century style, with some of Wordsworth's own personal effects.

Other famous names associated with Cockermouth include the mutineer on *The Bounty*, Fletcher Christian, Mary, Queen of Scots and Robert the Bruce.

The town now houses a printing museum, an art gallery at Castlegate House and Jennings' Brewery, which dates from 1828 and offers hour-long guided tours.

EGREMONT   MAP REF NY0110

With the River Ehen winding past it, and a wide main street lined with trees (and with a variety of stalls on its Friday market day), Egremont is a pretty town renowned as the home of ugly faces. For it is here that the World Gurning Championships are held each September. The country fair in which they take place is almost as old as Egremont Castle, whose ruins stand in a park on a hilltop overlooking that wide main street. This Norman building of red sandstone dates from the 12th century, though it was largely destroyed in the 16th century; its best surviving feature is the original gatehouse.

Dating from the 16th century is the Lowes Court Gallery on Main Street.

■ Visit

LOCAL SPECIALITIES

The crabs at the Egremont Crab Fair are crab apples not crustaceans. The fair dates from 1267, and on the third Saturday in September the Apple Cart parade passes through the town, and apples are thrown to people lining the route. Today they are eating apples, not crab apples. There are athletics competitions, animal shows, hound trails and a greasy pole competition. In the evening is the event that everyone knows about – the World Gurning Championship. It is more accurately called the 'Gurning through a Braffin' competition, and whoever can make the ugliest grin (gurn) while peering through a horse collar (a braffin), is declared world champion.

The gallery was restored for the promotion of local arts and crafts. Jewellery made from haematite – iron ore, can be bought in many craft and gift shops around the Lake District. Much of it came from Europe's last deep working iron ore mine, on the edge of Egremont. Florence Mine continued operating into the 21st century as a two-man enterprise, but finally succumbed to progress in 2009 when an arrangement it had with the nearby Sellafield site to pump water from the workings ended.

ENNERDALE MAP REF NY1015

Walkers may appreciate Ennerdale Water more than many other lakes, as access by car is limited and the bulk of its shores can only be explored on foot. Lying in the secluded valley of Ennerdale, its shores are well worth exploring – from the car park at

Bowness Knott, a path leads east along the forested northern side of the lake. The land around Ennerdale Water was bought by the Forestry Commission in 1926, and planting began the following year. Behind the rows of spruce and larch, the land rises steeply, to over 2,600 feet (793m) in places. Looking south the hills are higher still, with Pillar at 2,926 feet (892m), in front of which stands Pillar Rock – popular with climbers since its first ascent in 1826.

Ennerdale Water is actually a reservoir serving west Cumbria, and it is possible to walk all the way round, although the going can be tough and the whole route is 8 miles (12.8km) long.

GREAT GABLE MAP REF NY2110

There are higher mountains than Great Gable 2,949 feet (899m), but visually it holds its own. If approaching from the southwest from Wast Water and through Wasdale Head, its bulk resembles the great gable end of a house. This visually imposing approach, which is tough but accessible to fit walkers, is one route up to the top. Another option is from the northeast, from Seathwaite Farm climbing up past the waters of the Sourmilk Gill and passing Great Gable's little brother, Green Gable.

At the top a plaque proudly records the occasion when the surrounding area was given to the National Trust by the Fell and Rock Climbing Club, in memory of their colleagues lost in the First World War. A memorial service is held here each year on Remembrance Sunday.

It was also in these hills that you can see that modern climbing first started to develop, late in the 19th century. The names alone are inspiring: Needle Ridge, Eagle's Nest Ridge, Windy Gap. The view still inspires, south to Scafell Pike (3,210 feet/978m) and straight down Wasdale towards the Irish Sea.

LORTON MAP REF NY1625

Lorton Vale is the valley that sweeps south from Cockermouth and passes the village of Loweswater, Crummock Water and finally Buttermere before ending in the lofty Honister Pass. Five miles (8km) southeast of Cockermouth is the village of Lorton, which is divided in two. High Lorton clings to the side of Kirk Fell at the start of the Whinlatter Pass, and is famous for its yew tree. This magnificent tree which stands behind the village hall (known as Yew Tree Hall, of course) was described by Wordsworth in his poem, 'Yew Trees'. It is further celebrated because it was beneath its boughs that the founder of the Quaker movement, George Fox, preached to a large crowd under the watchful eyes of Cromwell's soldiers. At Whinlatter there is a Forestry Commission Visitor Centre, where you can watch the local ospreys on CCTV and discover more about this vast forest.

LOWESWATER MAP REF NY1221

One of the smaller lakes but is no less delightful for that, Loweswater is often less crowded than those lakes of easier access. To reach it involves a short drive on the B5289 down Lorton Vale from Cockermouth, but many motorists continue down the main road that leads to Crummock Water and Buttermere. Instead, take a turning through

Brackenthwaite, which leads along the north shore of the lake with parking at either end. Loweswater village is little more than a church, a village hall and a pub, with a scattering of whitewashed farm buildings surrounded by woodland and meadows. The woods offer many leafy footpaths and are cared for by the National Trust.

MARYPORT MAP REF NY0336

A comparatively new Cumbrian town, it was founded in 1749, Maryport was intended to serve as a port for the coal trade and was named after Mary, the wife of the Lord of the Manor, Humphrey Senhouse II. The port quickly grew, and for a short while was the biggest port in Cumberland, with trade from the coal and iron-ore mines and also a healthy shipbuilding industry.

The story of its rise and subsequent decline is told in the Maryport Maritime Museum, which also has exhibits ranging from a whale's tooth to telescopes. The museum is in Senhouse Street, which leads to Elizabeth Dock. Also by the quayside is the Lake District Coast Aquarium, which displays a surprising range of native marine and freshwater fish. On the hill above the town, the Senhouse Roman Museum has collections dating from 1570, when John Senhouse rescued some pieces from Maryport's Roman fort. It was added to by the family over the centuries, with some fine examples of Roman altars, and these are now on show in the Battery, an old naval building overlooking the Promenade and the Solway Firth.

From the Mouth of the Crooked River

This tour starts at Cockermouth, famous as the birthplace of Wordsworth. It continues to the coast at Maryport, before heading north, hugging the coastline and passing through small fishing villages and an Area of Outstanding Natural Beauty. The route then turns inland, taking in small villages and pretty market towns, crossing the boundary of the National Park and finally returning to Cockermouth.

Route Directions

In Cockermouth walk around and breathe in some of its character – visit Wordsworth House (the poet's birthplace) in Main Street. The 13th-century Norman castle is now partially ruined but a section is still inhabited by the Egremont family; however, the castle is rarely open.

1 Take the A594 out of Cockermouth and drive for 7 miles (11.2km) to Maryport. A port in Roman times, Maryport was developed in the 18th century by Humphrey Senhouse. Visit the harbour, marina, Maritime Museum and Aquarium, then go up the hill to the Roman Museum and look out over the town.

2 Leave Maryport on the A596 Carlisle road, turn left on the B5300 and continue ahead for 2 miles (3.2km) to a car park on the right for the saltpans. This was the site of a Roman milecastle.

3 Continue to Allonby. Allonby retains much of

its appeal from its days as a Georgian and Victorian bathing resort. Just across the Solway is Scotland and the Galloway hills.

4 From Allonby go north for 6 miles (9.6km) on the B5300 to Silloth. Until 1857 Silloth was a fishing village; it expanded as a port when linked by rail with Carlisle; the town still preserves its charming Victorian spa atmosphere.

5 Continue straight on past the green and drive for about 1.5 miles (2.4km) to Skinburness. This is a designated Area of Outstanding Natural Beauty.

6 Drive on a narrow road from Skinburness for another 2 miles (3.2km). Turn left on to the B5302 and go through Calvo to Abbeytown. The town was the site of Holme Cultram Abbey. Some of its buildings survived to become the splendid parish church. Robert the Bruce's

father was buried here in 1294, 25 years before his son sacked the abbey.

7 Leave Abbeytown on the B5302, then just beyond Waverbridge turn left on to an unclassified road, signed 'Aikhead and Station Hill'. On reaching the A596, turn left, then right into Wigton and then right again into the town centre. A feature of this town is the gilded granite fountain, erected in the 19th century. It shows four fine bronze reliefs of the *Acts of Mercy*.

8 Leave Wigton by going left in the town centre signed B5305 and then soon B5304. After about a mile (1.6km) cross the A595 and the continue ahead for 7 miles (11.3km) on an unclassified road, to arrive in Caldbeck on the B5299. To visit the village, park in the car park by the bridge and walk beside the river to a little bridge giving access to the Church of St Kentigern.

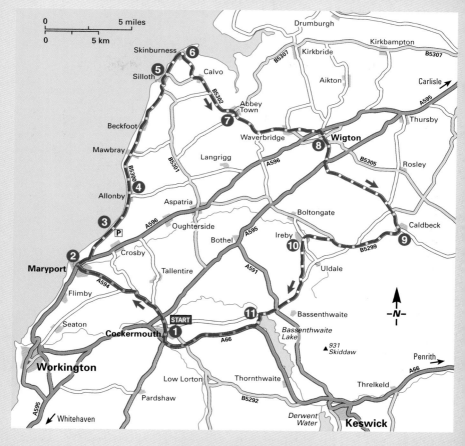

9 Leave Caldbeck in the same direction by which you entered the town, but bear left onto the B5299 (to the left of the Oddfellow's Arms). After driving for about 3 miles (5km), at a fork keep to the B5299 and then continue for another mile (1.6km) to a sign for Ireby. Turn left and then descend into the village, turn left again and follow the signs for Bassenthwaite. Here you enter the Lake District National Park.

10 Continue to a junction where a road from Uldale comes in on the left. Continue down to meet the A5291. Turn right, then left in front of the Castle Inn Hotel on to the B591. Keep ahead on the B5291, cross Ouse Bridge and turn left to a parking area. This is good place to stop and take a a stroll.

11 Keep on the B5291 for about half a mile (800m) to meet the A66, turn right and drive back along it to reach Cockermouth.

Wild Ennerdale

A superb ride through the forest beyond Ennerdale Water. This route, entering the heart of the high fells, joins the world of the mountaineer, the fell-runner and the long-distance walker.

Route Directions

1 Turn left from the car park, rolling down to the shores of Ennerdale Water. The track runs beside the lake for about 1 mile (1.6km), then continues through the forest above the river, here called Char Dub. 'Dub' is a common dialect word for a pool, while 'char' refers to a species of fish. Continue past Low Gillerthwaite Field Centre and then the youth hostel at High Gillerthwaite.

2 Just past the youth hostel the track forks. Keep right (really straight ahead). The track goes up and down more than you might expect. Take care on fast downhill bends where the surface is loose. Above all, don't grab the brakes. At the next fork 1 mile (1.6km) further on, a sign to the right points to Pillar. Save the Pillar road for the return and keep straight on – in fact, this track straight ahead gives the best views of the Pillar Rock. The way climbs gradually to a more level stretch with open views across the valley to Pillar

directly opposite. Pillar Rock is the centrepiece of a mass of crags strewn across the north face of the mountain. At this point you could turn back.

3 As Pillar falls behind, the valley head opens up. There's a space where you may find vehicles and then the main track curves down right.

4 Straight ahead through a gate is a much rougher track leading 400yds (366m) to Black Sail Hut – many people may prefer to walk for some or all of it. You can make yourself tea or coffee (leave a suitable donation). Return to the gate. The bridleway going up right climbs to Scarth Gap Pass and then descends to Buttermere. Ignore it, and go back through the gate and down left to the River Liza.

5 Splash through the ford and swing round right. Now keep straight ahead along the track, mostly downhill, ignoring branches off the track up and left until it swings down to the river.

Route facts

DISTANCE/TIME
12 miles (19.3km) 2h

MAP OS Explorer OL4 The English Lakes (NW)

START Bowness Knott car park; grid ref: NY 109153

TRACKS Good forest roads, occasionally bumpy

GETTTING TO THE START
The car park is half way along the north shore of Ennerdale Water, at a dead-end. Access is via minor roads east from Ennerdale Bridge or south from Lamplugh.

THE PUB Shepherd's Arms Hotel, Ennerdale Bridge. Tel: 01946 861249; www.shepherdsarmshotel. co.uk

❶ Rough track on the last short section (400yds/366m) to Black Sail Hut – mountain bike and some skill needed, or walk. Suitability: children 10+. Younger children will enjoy a shorter version

6 Cross the bridge and go up to the 'Pillar' signpost. Rejoin the main track of the outward route to return to your car at the car park.

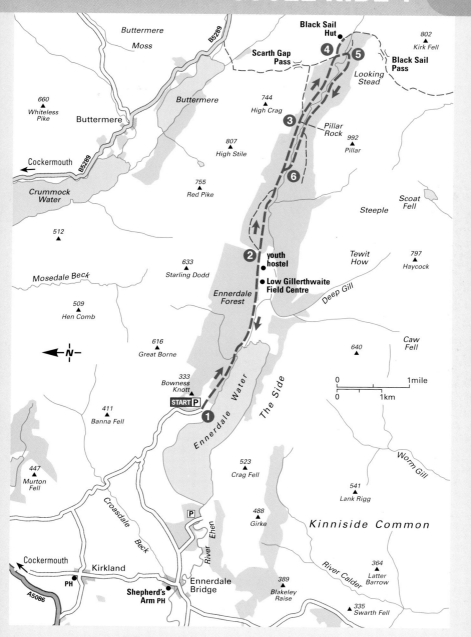

Buttermere
Moss

B5289

Black Sail
Hut

Scarth Gap
Pass

4

5

Black Sail
Pass

802 ▲
Kirk Fell

Looking
Stead

660 ▲
Whiteless
Pike

Buttermere

Buttermere

744 ▲
High Crag

Pillar
Rock

992 ▲
Pillar

Cockermouth

B5289

3

807 ▲
High Stile

Crummock
Water

755 ▲
Red Pike

6

Scoat
Fell

512 ▲

Steeple

Tewit
How

797 ▲
Haycock

Mosedale Beck

633 ▲
Starling Dodd

2

youth
hostel

Low Gillerthwaite
Field Centre

Deep Gill

509 ▲
Hen Comb

Ennerdale
Forest

616 ▲
Great Borne

Caw
Fell

640 ▲

N

333 ▲
Bowness
Knott

START P

1

Ennerdale Water

The Side

0 ——— 1mile
0 ——— 1km

411 ▲
Banna Fell

523 ▲
Crag Fell

447 ▲
Murton
Fell

541 ▲
Lank Rigg

Croasdale Beck

P

River Ehen

488 ▲
Girke

Kinniside Common

Worm Gill

Cockermouth

Kirkland

PH

A5086

Ennerdale
Bridge

**Shepherd's
Arm PH**

389 ▲
Blakeley
Raise

River Calder

364 ▲
Latter
Barrow

335 ▲
Swarth Fell

ST BEES MAP REF NX9711

St Bees is the start of Wainwright's famous 190-mile (304km) Coast-to-Coast walk to Robin Hood's Bay in North Yorkshire, not to mention a coast-to-coast cycle route. Popular with walkers, therefore, it is a pleasant village in which to linger before heading off to the east. Before you go inland, take time to explore the impressive sandstone cliffs of St Bees Head, which rise to 462 feet (141m) and which lead to the lighthouse looking over Saltom Bay towards Whitehaven. This part of the coast is Cumbria's only Heritage Coast, with land on the cliffs forming the St Bees Head Nature Reserve. Watch out for puffins, razorbills and kittiwakes, as well as the black guillemot, which breeds nowhere else in England.

In the village itself is the Church of Saint Mary and Saint Bega, which dates back to about AD 650, when it was part of a priory. St Bees also has its own beach, with several other beaches south along the coast. Six miles (9.6km) southeast of St Bees is the Sellafield Nuclear Site and its Visitor Centre, where visitors are treated to a series of displays explaining the Sellafield story and the virtues of nuclear power.

WHITEHAVEN MAP REF NX9718

In the middle of the 18th century Whitehaven was the third largest port in Britain, after London and Bristol, thanks to the local industries. Today, Whitehaven has a small fishing fleet, and its harbour is a conservation area, with several monuments to its past mining history, which finally died out in 1986.

Your first stop in Whitehaven should be The Beacon, on West Strand, which offers visitors an insight into the history of the town and harbour using audio-visual presentations and exciting displays. On the top floor is the Weather Gallery full of high-tech equipment that monitors and records the weather. On the headland above The Beacon is the winding gear and engine house of the Haig Colliery Mining Museum. Haig was the town's last deep pit, bringing coal from several miles under the sea. Now it records the often tragic stories of the town's mining past, in which more than 1,200 men, women and children died.

The town boasts many handsome Georgian buildings and has two churches that are worth seeking out. St Begh's dates from around 1868 and is visually striking as it was built from white stone with a red stone dressing. St James' is slightly older, from 1753, with Italian ceiling designs and a very moving Memorial Chapel. It was dedicated first to those who lost their lives in the two World Wars, and later also to local people who were killed in mining accidents. A miner's lamp serves as the Sanctuary lamp. At night, the bridge across the marina is lit up to dramatic effect.

Book lovers should note that Whitehaven has the largest antiquarian bookshop in Cumbria, and one of the largest in the north of England. Michael Moon's Antiquarian Bookshop in Lowther Street claims to have 100,000 books on its mile (1.6km) of shelving, on two floors, with room for at least a hundred contented book browsers.

Loweswater

You will discover the Lakeland's finest natural balcony path in this little-trodden corner of the northwestern Fells – green, flat and true – and with wonderful views across the lake to Darling Fell. Loweswater is a little remote from the more popular parts of Lakeland so not surprisingly, it is one of the finest, yet least talked about Lakes, although it is celebrated among anglers for its trout and perch. It is also a bit of a thief: it steals the best views of Crummock Water fells – Grasmoor and Whiteside never looked more fair than they do from Carling Knott's balcony path, and Mellbreak bursts into the sky like a volcano – steep, serious and rocky.

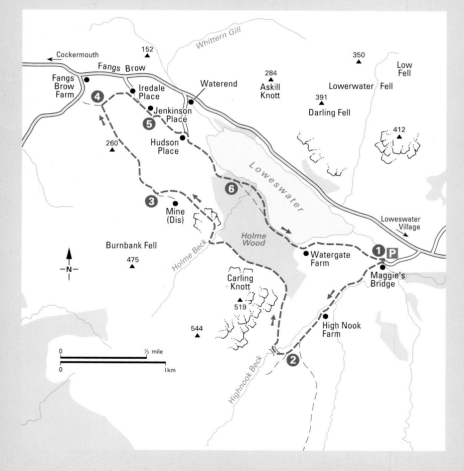

Route Directions

1 Just opposite the car park entrance go through the gate to High Nook Farm and follow the track through the fields. After passing through the farmyard continue along a stony track that climbs into the comb of Highnook Beck and beneath the craggy sides of Carling Knott.

2 Take the right fork each time the path divides. This will bring you down to the footbridge across the beck. Over the bridge the route continues as a fine grassy track that doubles back right, raking across the hillside to the top of the Holme Wood plantations. The track follows the top edge of the woods before traversing the breast of Burnbank Fell.

3 The track swings left and climbs to a ladder stile and a gate to the north of the fell. Here it divides. Ignore the left fork, which doubles back to an old mine. Instead go over the stile and descend gradually northwest across high pastureland.

4 A couple of hundred paces short of the road, at Fangs Brow, turn right over a ladder stile and then continue along a rutted track past Iredale Place farm. Just beyond the house the track joins a tarmac lane.

5 Beyond Jenkinson Place (a farm) the tarmac lane ends. Turn left here, over a stile and follow a well-defined grass track across the fields towards Hudson Place and the lake. A signpost diverts the way left, around the farm complex. The path meets a lane from Waterend farm. Turn right and follow the lane, which becomes a track near the shores of Loweswater before entering Holme Wood.

6 A wide track now heads through the woods, but by taking a path to the left, you can get nearer the shoreline. This second path rejoins the original track just beyond a stone built bunkhouse. At Watergate Farm, turn left to follow a wide gravel road back to the car park at Maggie's Bridge.

Route facts

DISTANCE/TIME
5 miles (8km) 3h

MAP OS Explorer OL4
The English Lakes (NW)

START Maggie's Bridge car park, Loweswater; grid ref: NY 134210

TRACKS Well-defined paths and tracks, all stiles have adjacent gates

GETTING TO THE START
Loweswater lies between the small Loweswater lake and the northern tip of Crummock Water. Maggie's Bridge car park (arrive early for a place) is down a very narrow lane, 0.5 mile (800m) west of the church and the Kirkstile Inn.

THE PUB Kirkstile Inn, Loweswater, 0.5 mile (800m) off route. Tel: 01900 85219; www.kirkstile.com

! Suitability: children 6+

■ TOURIST INFORMATION CENTRES

Cockermouth
The Town Hall.
Tel 01900 822634

Egremont
Lowes Court Gallery,
12 Main Street.
Tel 01946 820693

Maryport
Town Hall, Senhouse Street.
Tel 01900 812101

Whitehaven
Market Hall, Market Place.
Tel 01946 598914

Workington
Carnegie Theatre Foyer,
Finkle Street.
Tel 01900 606699

■ PLACES OF INTEREST

The Beacon
West Strand, Whitehaven.
Tel: 01946 592302

Castlegate House Gallery
Cockermouth.
Tel: 01900 822149. Free.

Haig Colliery Mining Museum
Kells, Whitehaven.
Tel: 01946 599949;
www.haigpit.com

Helena Thompson Museum
Park End Road, Workington.
Tel: 01900 606155. Free.

Jennings Brewery
Castle Brewery,
Cockermouth.
Tel: 0845 1297 185

Lake District Coast Aquarium
South Quay, Maryport.
Tel: 01900 817760

Lakeland Sheep and Wool Centre & Cumwest Visitor Centre
Egremont Road,
Cockermouth.
Tel: 01900 822673

Lowes Court Gallery
12 Main Street, Egremont.
Tel: 01946 820693.
Free.

Maryport Maritime Museum
1 Senhouse Street, Maryport.
Tel: 01900 813738

The Printing House
102 Main Street,
Cockermouth.
Tel: 01900 824984

The Rum Story
Lowther Street, Whitehaven.
Tel: 01946 592933

Sellafield Centre
Signposted off A595.
Tel: 01946 727027. Free.

Senhouse Roman Museum
The Battery, Sea Brows,
Maryport. Tel: 01900 816168

Wordsworth House
Main Street, Cockermouth.
Tel: 01900 824805

■ SHOPPING

Egremont
Market, Fri.

Maryport
Market, Fri.

Whitehaven
Market, Thu & Sat.
Michael Moon's Antiquarian
Bookshop
19 Lowther Street.
Tel: 01946 599010

Workington
Market, Wed & Sat.

LOCAL SPECIALITIES

Beer
Jennings beers.

Cumberland Rum Butter
Available in local shops.

■ PERFORMING ARTS

Carnegie Theatre and Arts Centre
Finkle Street,
Workington.
Tel: 01900 602122

Civic Hall
Whitehaven.
Tel: 01946 514960

Rosehill Theatre
Moresby, Whitehaven.
Tel: 01946 692422

■ OUTDOOR ACTIVITIES

ANGLING
Contact Tourist Information
Centres or the National Trust.
Tel: 01539 435599 (local NT)

Loweswater Water End Farm
Tel: 01946 861465

BEACHES

Allonby
Sand and shingle.

Beckfoot
Sand and shingle.

St Bees
Sand and shingle. Fleswick
Bay, shingle, sand at low
tide.

Silloth
Sand and shingle. Bathing
is not safe when the tide
is ebbing.

BOAT HIRE

Loweswater
Water End Farm.
Tel: 01946 861465

CYCLING

**Coast-to-Coast (C2C)
Cycle Route**
A 140-mile (224km) route
linking Whitehaven and
Workington to Sunderland.

The Reivers Cycle Route
A 190-mile (306km) route:
Tynemouth to Whitehaven.

Hadrian's Cycleway
National Cycle Route 72;
a 170-mile (274km) route.

West Cumbria Cycle Network
Routes on disused railways
and minor roads.

CYCLE HIRE

Cleator
Ainfield Cycles,
Jacktrees Road.
Tel: 01946 812427

Whitehaven
Haven Cycles, Preston Street.
Tel: 01946 63263

Wigton
Wigton Cycle & Sports,
23 West Street.
Tel: 01697 342824

GOLF COURSES

Cockermouth
Cockermouth Golf Club,
Embleton. Tel: 01768 76941

Maryport
Maryport Golf Club, Bank
End. Tel: 01900 812605

St Bees
St Bees Golf Club.
Tel: 01946 824300. (9-hole).

Seascale
Seascale Golf Club,
The Banks.
Tel: 01964 728202

Whitehaven
Whitehaven Golf Club,
Red Lonning.
Tel: 01946 591144

Workington
Workington Golf Club.
Tel: 01900 603460

HORSE-RIDING

Ennerdale
Bradley's, Low Cock How.
Tel: 01946 861354

Gilcrux
Allonby Riding School.
Tel: 01697 322889

LONG-DISTANCE FOOTPATHS & TRAILS

Coast-to-Coast Walk
A 190-mile (304km) walk
from St Bees Head to Robin
Hood's Bay, North Yorkshire.

The West Lakes Way
A 70-mile (112km) walk from
Whitehaven to Millom taking
in Scafell and Black Combe.

NATURE RESERVES

Contact local TIC or Solway
Coast Discovery Centre.
Tel: 01693 33055

SAILING

Crummock Water
Woodhouse, Buttermere.
Permits and boats for hire.
Tel: 01768 770208

Maryport
Maryport Marina.
Tel: 01900 814431

■ ANNUAL EVENTS & CUSTOMS

Broughton
Children's Carnival, early Jul.

Buttermere
Shepherds' Meet, mid-Sep.
Buttermere Show, late Oct.

Cockermouth
Cockermouth Sheepdog
Trials, mid-May.
Cockermouth Carnival, Jun.
Cockermouth Festival, Jul.
Cockermouth and District
Agricultural Show, late Jul.

Egremont
West Cumbria Rose Society
Show, late Jul.
Crab Fair and the World
Gurning Championship, Sep.

Ennerdale Bridge
Ennerdale and Kinniside
Agricultural Show, late Aug.

Lorton
Vale of Lorton Sheepdog
Trials, late Jul.

Loweswater
Loweswater and
Brackenthwaite Agricultural
Show, mid-Sep.

Maryport
Maryport and District
Carnival, early Jul.

Whitehaven
Whitehaven Festival, late Jun.

Workington
Curwen Fair, late May.

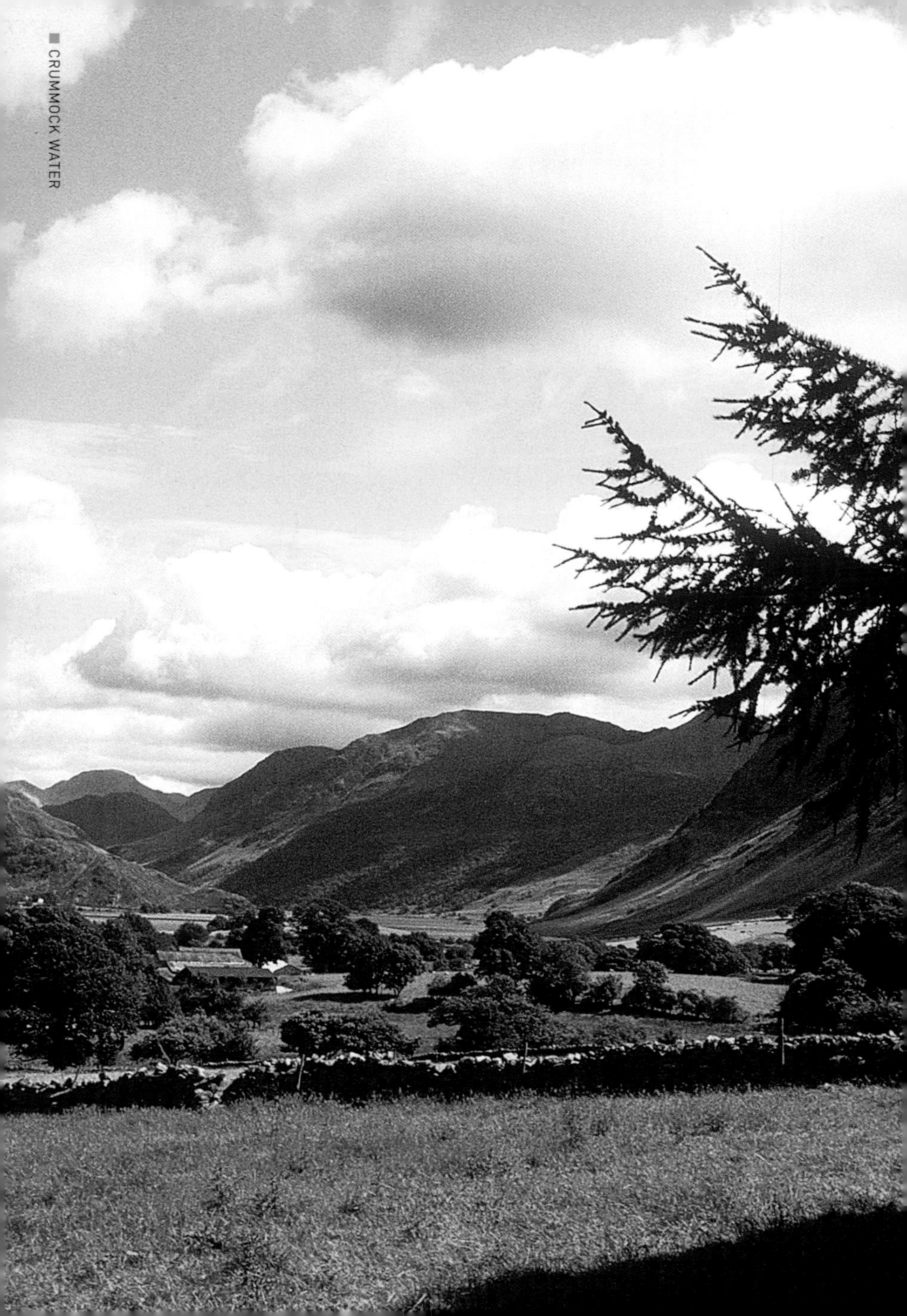

Tea Rooms

Syke Farm

Buttermere, Cockermouth CA13 9XA. Tel: 01768 770277

Ice cream is the speciality here, home-made with milk from the farm's resident herd of Ayrshire cattle. But this tiny tea room just below the little church is also great for home-made cakes, bakes and scones, and there's a little craft shop too.

Siskins Café

Whinlatter Forest Visitor Centre, Braithwaite, Keswick CA12 5TW Tel: 01768 778410

High up on the Whinlatter Pass, the Forest Visitor Centre and Siskins Café is a great base for exploring the surrounding woodland. From the balcony you can watch the never-ending stream of birds on strategically placed feeders, high in the trees in front of you.

The Gincase

Mawbray Hayrigg, Silloth, Wigton CA7 4LL Tel 01697 332020 www.gincase.co.uk

In a converted farm building, where once horses would have powered a grinding stone, the Gincase is a tea room, shop, art gallery and rare breed animal park. On warm days sit in the orchard and enjoy the home-baking in this very quiet spot just a mile or so from the sea.

Harbour Gallery and Café

The Beacon, West Strand, Whitehaven CA28 7LY Tel: 01946 592302 www.thebeaconwhitehaven. co.uk

After exploring Whitehaven's historic waterfront, unwind in the peaceful Harbour Gallery Café, surrounded by the artwork of local and community groups. Freshly made sandwiches and snacks are available as well as excellent cream teas. Admission to the adjacent Harbour Gallery is free.

Pubs

Fish Hotel

Buttermere, Cockermouth CA13 9XA Tel: 01768 770253 www.fishhotel.com

Once the home of Mary Robinson, the legendary Maid of Buttermere, the staff at the Fish Hotel pride themselves on understanding the needs of walkers, mountain climbers and fishermen. Beers include Hesket Newmarket's famous ales and tasty bar snacks are also available.

Kirkstile Inn

Loweswater, Cockermouth CA13 0RU Tel: 01900 85219 www.kirstileinn.com

With beams and low ceilings, stone floors, real open fires and real ales brewed on the premises this is, to many visitors, the idea of the perfect Lakeland pub. It's very popular with locals too, bringing an authenticity rarely found elsewhere. The food is also of a very high standard and accommodation is available.

Shepherd's Arms

Ennerdale Bridge, Cleator CA23 8AR Tel: 01946 861249 www.shepherdsarmshotel. co.uk

Located right in the centre of Ennerdale Bridge village this relaxed and informal free house serves Jennings' and Yates's beers. They do a very good line in vegetarian dishes, as well as some tasty creations using fish and locally sourced game, while the two open fires in autumn and winter make it very cosy. Local musicians sometimes play in the bar and the pub is a popular stopping point for weary walkers on the Alfred Wainwright Coast to Coast footpath.

Bassenthwaite & Borrowdale

Keswick is at the heart of the northern half of the Lake District. To the south are the wooded surrounds of Derwent Water, which lead to a narrow pass of volcanic rock, the Jaws of Borrowdale. To the north is the great hulk of Skiddaw, built up on softer, smoother slate.

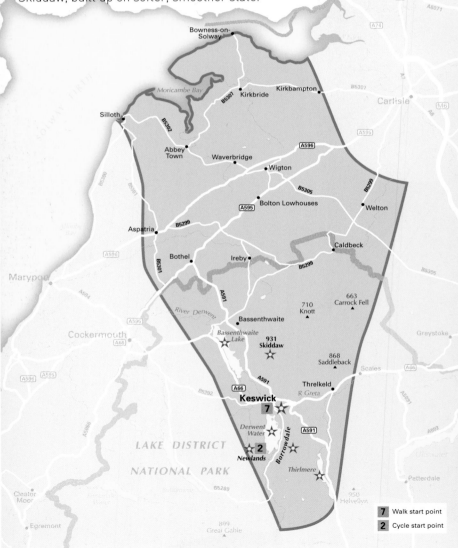

7 Walk start point

2 Cycle start point

DERWENT VALLEY

Unmissable attractions

If you're staying in Keswick, then Skiddaw is the peak to climb. From the top the views are marvellous. To the north are the Scottish mountains and in the far west the Isle of Man. The peaks of the Pennines rise towards the east, while all around are the Lakeland's other hills and dales. Derwent Water attractively dotted with islands, can be explored by one of the ferries that ply the stretches between the seven landing stages around the lake.

1

1 Castlerigg Stone Circle
Dating from the early Bronze Age, Castlerigg is one of the most imposing and probably one of the most spectacularly sited ancient monuments.

2 Derwent Water
Typical of everything that is beautiful in the Lake District, this broad lake is ringed by mountain peaks and dotted with mysterious tree-clad islands.

3 Newlands Valley
This area was once a thriving mining community. Remnants of the old, aptly named, Goldscope mine can be seen among the bracken of Scope End.

4 Keswick & Skiddaw
The Scottish hills, the Isle of Man and the Pennine peaks can be seen from the top of Skiddaw.

BASSENTHWAITE LAKE

MAP REF NY2026

Owned by the National Park, only quiet activities are permitted on the lake. It is important as a home for a rare fish, the Vendace, as well as for wintering wildfowl, and is designated as a Site of Special Scientific Interest and a National Nature Reserve. Bassenthwaite village is to the northeast, a short distance from the lake. Near the village, Trotters World of Animals is good for children.

Beside the A591 are the grounds of 17th-century Mirehouse, which lead down to the eastern shores of the lake and incorporate adventure playgrounds and a tea room set in the former sawmill. Nearby is the Norman Church of St Bega. It is an inspiring setting, with Skiddaw (3,054 feet/931m) rising in the east. The location by the lake certainly inspired Tennyson, a regular visitor, who described, in *Morte d'Arthur*, the dying King Arthur being carried across the waters of the lake on a barge, thus making Bassenthwaite Lake the last resting place of Excalibur. A waymarked walk in the grounds allows visitors to enjoy the lakeside scenery, and to watch for a sword rising out of the water!

Mirehouse has been in the same family since 1688. It has a wildflower meadow and a walled garden, while inside is a fine collection of furniture, literary portraits and manuscripts reflecting the family friendships with Tennyson, Wordsworth, artist Francis Bacon, Scottish historian and essayist Thomas Carlyle and Edward Fitzgerald, English poet and translator of *The Rubáiyát of Omar Khayyám*.

BORROWDALE

MAP REF NY2414

This glorious wooded valley, which runs south from Derwent Water, contains two of the Lake District's most dramatic natural features – the Bowder Stone and the Jaws of Borrowdale. The Stone is signposted along a path east of the B5289 Borrowdale road, south of the village of Grange. Why stop to look at a stone? Well this one weighs about 2,000 tons and appears to be balanced, ready to topple over. A set of steps leads up to the top of its 36 feet (11m), and despite the attempts of almost everyone who visits to give it a push, it hasn't fallen yet. It was put into place by a glacier, which later melted around it.

Here, too, are the so-called Jaws of Borrowdale, where the high crags on either side of the valley almost meet, squeezing the road and the river (the B5289 and the River Derwent) together as they both try to get through. Both do, and the road then swings round to the west, through the village of Seatoller, to climb through the equally dramatic Honister Pass, which links Borrowdale with Buttermere.

DERWENT WATER

MAP REF NY2519

South from Keswick spreads Derwent Water. It is the lakeland's widest lake at 1.25 miles (2km) and is attractively dotted with islands. These include, in the very centre, St Herbert's Island, named after the saint who lived here as a hermit in the 7th century. Derwent Isle was once home to German miners who came to work around Keswick and the

■ Visit

CASTLERIGG STONE CIRCLE

Just 2 miles (3.2km) east of Keswick is one of the most dramatic and atmospheric stone circles in Britain. It dates from about 2000 BC, but its purpose is unknown, adding to its enigmatic qualities. The 38 stones in the circle itself, with a further 10 set in the centre, are surrounded by high fells, with Helvellyn to the southeast. They are made of volcanic Borrowdale rock, brought here by the glaciers of the Ice Age. The construction is actually oval in shape, 107 feet (33m) across at its widest point, and the name means 'the fort on the ridge', though no evidence of any fort exists here. Castlerigg Stone Circle is in the hands of the National Trust.

Newlands Valley in the 16th century. With Borrowdale closing in to the south, and crags on either side of the lake's southern half, Derwent Water is a popular favourite. Popular too is the way in which it can be explored by using the ferries which run between the seven landing stages around the lake, allowing visitors to get off and walk the many footpaths through the surrounding woods and up to the various viewpoints. There are also good views from the high narrow road on the lake's western edge.

The eastern side is rich in waterfalls, such as the spectacular Lodore Falls in the southeastern corner, which is one of the stops for the ferries. Much of the land here is owned by the National Trust. This is largely due to the efforts of Canon Hardwicke Rawnsley, vicar of Crosthwaite, the parish church of Keswick. He was Secretary of the National Trust from its formation until his death in 1920. The beautiful Friar's Crag, on the northern shore of Derwent Water close to the Keswick boat landings, was given to the National Trust (along with Lords Island and Calf Close Bay) to be his memorial. The view from here was deemed by Ruskin 'to be one of the finest in Europe'.

KESWICK MAP REF NY2623

Keswick is a natural centre for mountain climbers, country walkers and more leisurely tourists alike. It is small, with a population of under 5,000, but is said, for its size, to have more beds for guests than anywhere else in the country. This gives an idea of what it can be like on a sunny Bank Holiday weekend.

If now reliant on tourism, in the past it was mining that kept it alive. The industry flourished in the 16th century with the formation, at the behest of Elizabeth I, of the Company of Mines Royal. Expert miners came from Germany and settled on Derwent Isle. But as the mining industry declined by the second half of the 19th century, so a new source of prosperity came in 1865 when the Cockermouth–Penrith railway line was built, bringing mass tourism.

Graphite is the reason the Cumberland Pencil Museum exists here today. A delightfully quirky specialist collection, it shows that even the humble pencil has a fascinating history. The first was made locally in the 1550s, though you can see modern production methods too, and the largest pencil in the world! Even if you are not mad on cars, you'll find that the Cars of the Stars

Motor Museum is a fascinating collection. Some are merely interesting vehicles, such as a Fiat from 1972 painted to look like the Noddy Car. The 'Star Cars' range from one of the Reliant Robins used in *Only Fools and Horses*, to a Morris 8 Tourer driven by James Herriot in *All Creatures Great and Small*, and a selection of cars used in the James Bond films, including several Aston Martins.

One of the oldest museums in the county is the Keswick Museum and Art Gallery, which has a good display on Lakeland's literary connections. This covers in particular the poet Robert Southey, who moved to Greta Hall in Keswick (now part of a school) to join his brother-in-law, Coleridge, and remained there for over 40 years until his death in 1843. He became Poet Laureate in 1813. There is also a fine period scale model of the Lake District as it was in the early 19th century and, even older, a 500-year-old mummified cat! The geology collection is of national importance and contains mineral examples from the Caldbeck Fells. Geology is also the key to the Keswick Mining Museum. As well as important mineral collections, there is an excellent bookshop for those interested in industrial archaeology.

On the northern edge of Keswick at Crosthwaite is the Church of St Kentigern, whose best-known incumbent, Canon Rawnsley, was the first Secretary of the National Trust. A friend of Beatrix Potter, he was also an author, journalist, educationalist and orator. His influence pervades almost every corner of Keswick and Cumbria.

NEWLANDS MAP REF NY2420

In the delightful Newlands Valley, with its rolling green fields, there is little evidence left today that this was once a busy industrial mining community. In fact you have to search hard to find any communities at all, as there are only a handful of farms and the two tiny hamlets of Little Town and Stair. Having found them, each will stake its own claim to fame. A farmhouse at Stair has the inscription 'TF 1647'. The initials are believed to be those of Thomas Fairfax, commander of the Parliamentary forces, who stayed here during the turmoil following the end of the Civil War in 1646. Little Town's fame could hardly be more different, as its name features in Beatrix Potter's *The Tale of Mrs Tiggywinkle*.

Copper and lead were mined on the valley's eastern slopes, and small deposits of silver and gold were also found there. Today the landscape has returned to nature, a beautiful, gentle and green landscape down in the valley, but rising up through a steep and rugged pass in the southwest before descending to Buttermere.

■ Insight

BEAR POET

Robert Southey (1774–1843) is perhaps the least known today of the Lakeland poets, despite the fact that he was Poet Laureate for 30 years. One of his works, however, has become such a well-known story that it is often believed to be a traditional fairy-tale. Not so. Robert Southey wrote the original story of *The Three Bears*, although the character of Goldilocks was a later anonymous embellishment.

Keswick's Walla Crag above Derwent Water

At the foot of Borrowdale – often referred to as the most beautiful valley in England – the northern head of Derwent Water opens to Keswick and the northern fells with dramatic effect. The highlight of this walk is undeniably the panoramic views from the heights of Walla Crag to the surrounding fells.

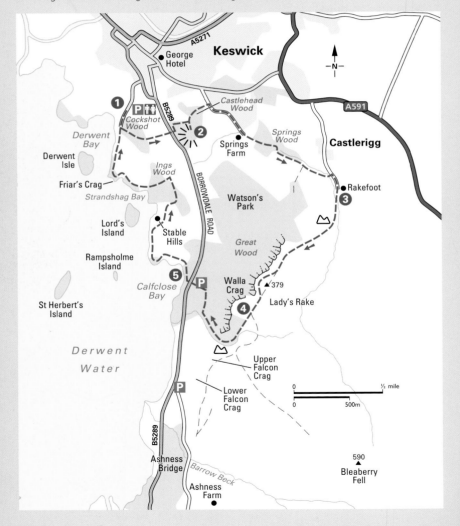

Route Directions

1 Proceed down the road to Derwent Bay. Go left opposite the landing stages, past the toilets, to take the track through Cockshot Wood. Exit the wood on to a fenced lane which leads across the field to the Borrowdale road. Cross the road and climb the stone steps to enter Castlehead Wood. Take the path which trends left to ascend the shoulder. In a little way a steeper path climbs up to the right, to the rocky summit of Castle Head and a fine viewpoint.

2 Descend by the same route to the shoulder then bear right to locate a kissing gate into an enclosed lane. Follow this to Springs Road and turn right. When you reach Springs Farm, cross a bridge and take the track up through Springs Wood. Bear right at the junction and follow the edge of the wood up past the TV mast. Ignore a turning on the right and continue to a footbridge left to join Castlerigg Road. Turn right along the road and walk up past Rakefoot to another footbridge on the right.

3 Cross the footbridge over the stream and follow the path, ascending by the stone wall. Go through a gate, and walk out on to the open shoulder of the fell, ascending the steep grassy nose. The going levels until a gate on the right, through the wall, leads to a path which follows the edge of the crag. Caution, there is a steep unfenced drop. Those wishing to stay away from the cliff edge can take a higher stile. Follow the path, which crosses the head of a gully, to climb on to the polished rock cap of Walla Crag where the views are superb.

4 Continue along the main ridge path down to a stile over the wall. Cross and go right, down the hill following a grassy path which becomes increasingly steep and stepped into the gorge of Cat Gill. Entering Great Wood continue steeply down, passing a bridge before leaving the beck to head into the wood. Bear left down the hill, across a wooded car park and on, to locate a gap in the wall on the Borrowdale Road. Cross to the gap in the wall opposite and continue to the lakeshore.

5 Bear right, following around Calfclose Bay, by Stable Hills, around Ings Wood and Strandshag Bay to the Scots pine on Friar's Crag. Continue easily back to Derwent Bay and take the footpath along the road to the car park.

Route facts

DISTANCE/TIME
5.25 miles (8.4km) 3h

MAP OS Explorer OL4 The English Lakes (NW)

START Lakeside car park, Keswick; grid ref: NY 265229

TRACKS Good paths and tracks, steep ascent and descent, 3 stiles

GETTING TO THE START
From central Keswick, take the B5289 Borrowdale Road at the western end of the town. Follow it for 600yds (549m) and turn right to reach the Lakeside car park.

THE PUB Lake Road Inn, Keswick, near start of route. Tel: 01768 772404

❶ Paths run close to steep, unfenced drops on Walla Crag (an alternative route avoiding these is suggested). Suitability: children 10+

SKIDDAW MAP REF NY2629

When the Lakes first began to attract tourists in numbers in the 19th century, it was to Keswick that many of them came, and the one peak they would all walk to was Skiddaw. It is not the most attractive ascent lower down, but even though it rises to 3,054 feet (931m) it is a safe and manageable climb of a little more than two hours. You can even avoid the first 1,000 feet (305m) by parking at grid reference NY281254 above the village of Applethwaite, north of Keswick off the A591, and start the climb there. In both places the path to Skiddaw is clearly signed. At peak times walkers will be going up in droves, so this isn't a walk for those seeking solitude.

The rewards are at the top, however, even if you do have to share them. To the north are the Scottish mountains, and in the far west is the Isle of Man. The Pennine peaks rise towards the east, while all around are Lakeland's other hills and dales. If you want to escape the crowds then take the Cumbria Way, which circles behind the main peak into the area known as 'Back o' Skiddaw'.

THIRLMERE MAP REF NY3116

The A591 runs along the eastern side of the long thin lake of Thirlmere, with a car park near Wythburn chapel, built in the 17th century, at the southern end. From here a track leads up to Helvellyn, and before 1879 many a path would have led downwards, too. For the chapel is all that remains of Wythburn village, flooded in the 1890s when Thirlmere was dammed at the northern end and turned into Manchester's first Lakeland

■ **Insight**

ONLY HALF WAY UP

Charles Brown, friend and biographer of the poet John Keats, accompanied him in 1818 on a walking tour. In his journal Brown wrote of their climb up Skiddaw from Keswick; this extract shows that walking up mountains is the same for everyone: 'A promising morning authorised a guide to call us up at four o'clock, in order to ascend Skiddaw. The distance to the summit from the town is a little more than 6 miles (9.6km). Its height, from the level of the sea, is 3,022 feet (922m); but only 1,952 feet (595m) above Derwent Water – so lofty is all this part of the country. Helvellyn and Skawfell are somewhat higher, but the view from Skiddaw is esteemed the best. In a short time the continued steep became fatiguing; and then, while looking upward to what I thought was no very great distance from the top, it sounded like cruelty to hear from our guide that we were exactly half way!'

reservoir. Armboth in the northwest is also now beneath the waters, along with several farms on the shores of the original lake.

Thirlmere, an attractive, tree-fringed expanse, is one of the few lakes that can be driven, as well as walked, around. A minor road runs down the western edge, a lovely drive through the lakeside woods with several car parks, each with forest trails leading off from them. One trail leads north up to the summit of Raven Crag, and good views are also to be had half-way down the western edge at Hause Point, where the lake was once narrow enough to have had a bridge running across to the other side.

Meandering in Newlands Valley

Though close to Keswick's bustle, the Newlands Valley lacks any major visitor attractions and is still rural enough for visitors to be able to slip back into an easier pace of life. This classic Lakeland cycle route in Newlands Valley, west of Derwent Water, is surrounded by scenery that, even by Lakeland standards, is stunning, although you'll only catch glimpses of only one lake – Bassenthwaite.

Route Directions

1 From the parking place head up the steep hill to Little Town. Once through Little Town, relax and enjoy a fine winding, mostly downhill, run through the valley to Stair and a junction at the bottom of a hill.

2 Turn sharp right on to a narrow lane. The sign, half-hidden by vegetation, says 'Skelgill – Narrow

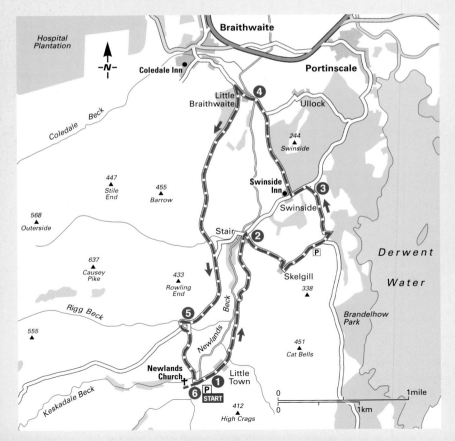

Gated Road'. Climb again, not too steeply, with the hill of Cat Bells ahead. The lane steepens as it twists through the tiny hamlet of Skelgill, reaching a gate just above. The gate forces a stop, and it is the top of the climb, so a good place for a look around. To the left of the isolated Swinside Hill, to the north, the stretch of water you can see is Bassenthwaite Lake. The lane passes a small parking area before reaching a T-junction on a bend. Turn left, downhill, over a cattle-grid and round another sharp bend. There'll usually be lots of parked cars here as it's the start of the main route up Cat Bells. The road levels out, then climbs to a junction.

3 Go left; the junction proves to be triangular. Go left again. As the road swings round to the right there are fantastic views up the valley and to the surrounding fells: Dale Head, Hindscarth, Maiden Moor and Robinson. Just beyond is the Swinside Inn. Turn right beside the pub on a narrow lane signed to Ullock and Braithwaite. Keep left where a road branches right to Ullock.

4 Cross a stone-arched bridge over Newlands Beck and begin a short climb, steep at the start. As it levels

out there's another fleeting glimpse of Bassenthwaite Lake. At a T-junction turn sharp left. The road runs south, generally level along the base of the steep slopes, and just high enough above the valley floor to give open views. Dip down to a small bridge. Just beyond is the start of the principal walkers' path up Causey Pike; you may well see figures struggling up the initial steep slope of Rowling End. A little further on, keep straight on past a sharp left turn (for Stair, Portinscale and Grange). For a little while the views are blocked by trees, mostly beech and larch, before the classic scene of the dale head begins to open up.

5 Very shortly, a steep stony track drops off to the left to a ford. Those seeking a moment's mountain-bike excitement can choose this track – it merely cuts off a short corner of the road. Alternatively, continue more sedately, round over a bridge to a wooden house. Turn left (signed to Newlands Church, Little Town) and drop down, then swing round, heading straight up the valley with its glorious range of fells ahead.

6 As you come right down into the valley bottom, turn

Route facts

DISTANCE/TIME 7 miles (11.3 km) 1h15

MAP OS Explorer OL4 The English Lakes (NW)

START Near Little Town, south of Skelgill; grid ref: NY 232194

TRACKS Lanes, mostly quiet

GETTING TO THE START Little Town is a hamlet between Buttermere and Derwent Water, on a narrow lane 4 miles (6.4km) south of Braithwaite. Roadside parking is at the bottom of the hill, just southwest of Little Town.

THE PUB Swinside Inn, Newlands, see Point 3 on route. Tel: 01768 778253; www.theswinsideinn.com

❶ Some ups and downs, but not too severe. Suitability: children 8+

right on the no-through-road to Newlands Church – closer even than the advertised 0.25 mile (400m). Retrace your route to the last junction and turn right, where it's only a few more pedal strokes to the bridge and the car park just beyond.

■ TOURIST INFORMATION CENTRES

Keswick
Moot Hall, Market Square.
Tel: 01768 772645

Silloth
Solway Coast Discovery Centre, Liddle Street.
Tel: 01697 331944

■ PLACES OF INTEREST

Cars of the Stars Motor Museum
Standish Street, Keswick.
Tel: 01768 773757.
Vehicles from television and film.

Castlerigg Stone Circle
2 miles (3.2km) east of Keswick. Free.

Cumberland Pencil Museum
Southey Works, Carding Mill Lane, Keswick.
Tel: 01768 773626
Displays of the history of the pencil and details of modern production methods.

Honister Slate Mine
Honister Pass.
Tel: 01768 777230
Guided working mine underground tours showing methods that have changed little over the past 300 years.

Keswick Mining Museum
Otley Road.
Tel: 01768 780055
Mining memorabilia and an exceptional bookshop devoted to geology and industrial archaeology.

Keswick Museum and Art Gallery
Fitz Park, Station Road, Keswick. Tel: 01768 773263
Displays of letters and manuscripts; also local geology and natural history.

Mirehouse
Three miles (4.6km) north of Keswick, off the A591.
Tel: 01786 772287
Seventeenth-century house where Tennyson wrote *Morte d'Arthur*. Walled garden, lakeside walks, four adventure playgrounds.

Solway Coast Discovery Centre
Liddle Street, Silloth.
Tel: 01697 333055
www.solwaycoastaonb.org.uk
Interpreting 10,000 years of the Solway's history.

Threlkeld Quarry and Mining Museum
Threlkeld, near Keswick.
Tel: 01768 779747.
Exhibits in a former quarry illustrate all aspects of Cumbrian mining, quarrying and geology.

Whinlatter Forest Visitor Centre
Whinlatter Forest Park, near Keswick. Tel: 01768 778469
Viewing points for local ospreys and other birds as well as interactive displays, walking and cycling trails and an adventure play area. Free.

■ FOR CHILDREN

Trotters World of Animals
Coalbeck Farm, Bassenthwaite, Keswick.
Tel: 01768 776239;
www.trottersworld.com.
A small, conservation-orientated zoo, with feeding displays and a soft play area.

■ SHOPPING

Keswick
Market, Sat.

Silloth
Market, Thu & Sat.

LOCAL SPECIALITIES

Allerdale and Cumberland Cheeses
Available from Booths, Tithebarn Street, Keswick.

Silloth Shrimps
Available from local fishmongers.

Solway Firth Salmon
Available from local fishmongers.

Sweet Cumberland Ham
Available from local butchers.

■ PERFORMING ARTS

Theatre by the Lake
Lakeside, Keswick.
Tel: 01768 774411

■ OUTDOOR ACTIVITIES

ANGLING

Bassenthwaite Lake
Permits from Keswick TIC or Pheasant Inn.
Tel: 01768 776234

Derwent Water
Permits from Keswick TIC.

Watendlath Tarn and Borrowdale Fisheries
Tel 01768 777293

BOAT HIRE

Derwent Water
Derwent Water Marina, Portinscale.
Tel: 01768 772912
Keswick Launch.
Tel: 01768 772263
Nichol End Marine, Portinscale.
Tel: 01768 773082

BOAT TRIPS

Derwent Water
Regular passenger service. Keswick Launch.
Tel: 01768 772263

CYCLE HIRE

Keswick
Keswick Motor Co, Lake Road.
Tel: 01768 772064
Keswick Mountain Bike Centre, Southey Hill Estate.
Tel: 01768 775202

GOLF COURSES

Aspatria
Brayton Park Golf Club, Brayton Park.
Tel: 01697 320840

Cockermouth
Cockermouth Golf Club, Embleton.
Tel: 01768 776223

Keswick
Keswick Golf Club, Threlkeld Hall.
Tel: 01768 779324

Silloth
Silloth-on-Solway Golf Club, The Clubhouse.
Tel: 01697 331304

HORSE-RIDING

Troutbeck, Penrith
Rookin House Farm.
Tel: 01768 483561

LONG-DISTANCE FOOTPATHS AND TRAILS

The Allerdale Ramble
A 55-mile (88km) walk from the Borrowdale valley to Silloth.

The Cumbria Coastal Way
A 124-mile (198.4km) walk from Milnthorpe to Carlisle.

SAILING

Bassenthwaite
Bassenthwaite Sailing Club.
Tel: 01768 776341

Derwent Water
Derwent Water Marina.
Tel: 01768 772912
Platty Plus, Lodore Boat Landing. Tel: 01768 776572
Nichol End Marine.
Tel: 01768 773082

WATERSPORTS

Derwent Water
Derwent Water Marina, Portinscale.
Tel: 01768 772912
Canoeing and windsurfing.
Nichol End Marine.
Tel: 01768 773082
Platty Plus, Lodore Boat Landing. Canoeing and windsurfing are available.
Tel: 01768 776572

■ ANNUAL EVENTS & CUSTOMS

Bassenthwaite
Regatta Week, early Aug.

Borrowdale
Borrowdale Shepherds' Meet and Show, mid-Sep.

Caldbeck
Caldbeck and Hesket Newmarket Sheepdog Trials, late Aug.
Hesket Newmarket Show, early Sep.

Cockermouth
Agricultural Show, late Jul.

Keswick
Keswick Literature Festival, Mar.
Keswick Jazz Festival, mid-May.
Keswick Mountain Festival, May.
Keswick Convention, mid to late Jul.
Keswick Victorian Fair, early Dec.

Silloth
Kite Festival, late Jul.
Silloth Carnival, August Bank Holiday.
Solfest, late Aug.

Threlkeld
Threlkeld Sheepdog Trials, mid-Aug.

Uldale
Uldale Shepherds' Meet and Blencathra Hunt, early Dec.

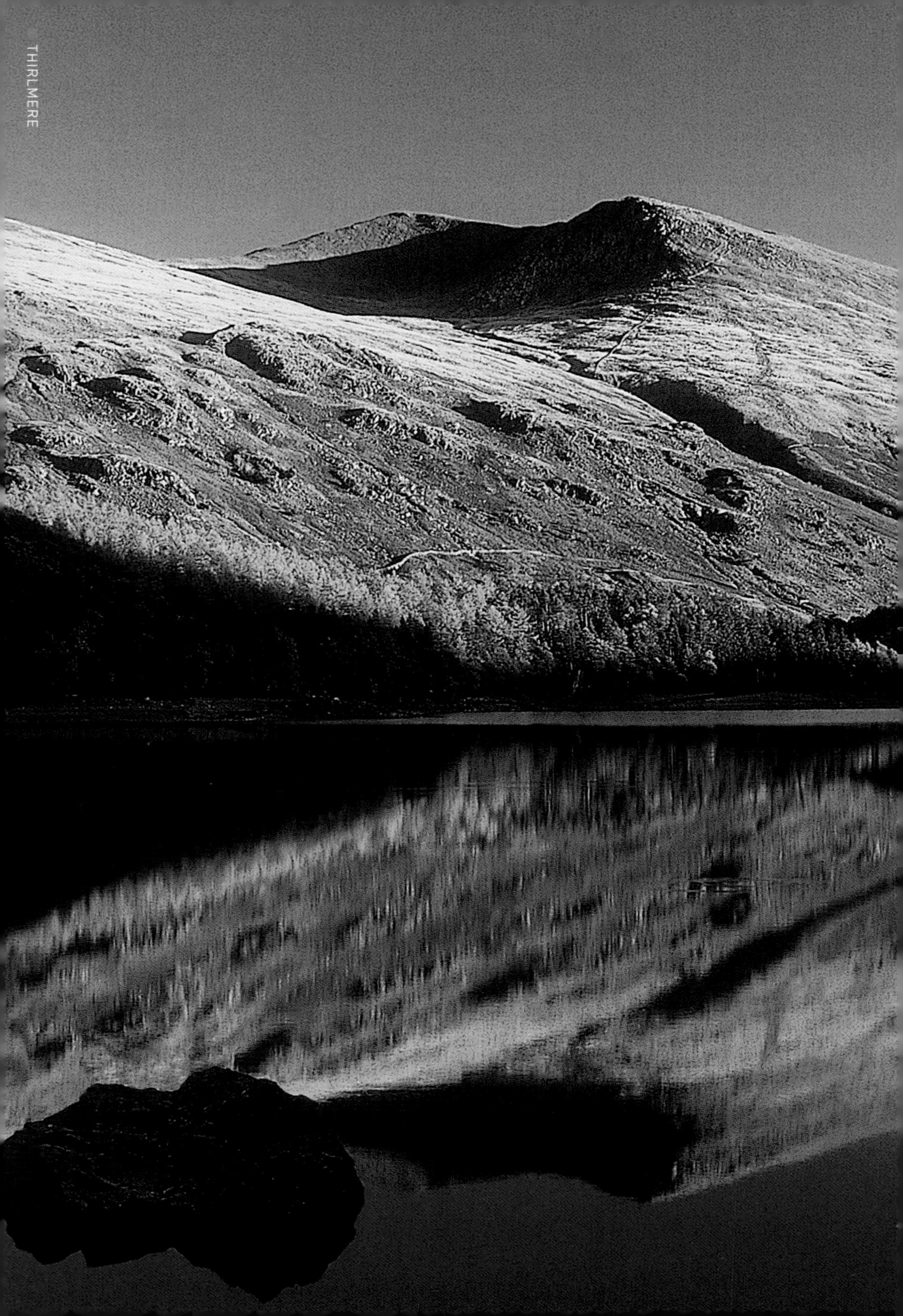

THIRLMERE

Tea Rooms

The Watermill Café
Priest's Mill,
Caldbeck CA7 8DR
Tel: 01697 478267
www.watermillcafe.co.uk
Overlooking the River Caldew, this beautifully restored monastic mill site houses craft shops as well as the Watermill Café. Fairtrade and vegetarian options are a speciality and on warmer days you can sit on the terrace, which also overlooks the village cricket pitch.

Flock In
Yew Tree Farm, Rosthwaite,
Borrowdale CA12 5XB
Tel: 01768 777675
On a working fell farm in Borrowdale, it's no surprise that the local Herdwick lamb crops up in many of the snacks on offer here. Royal patronage may have helped raise the profile of this diversification project, but the tea bread and shortbread are seriously tasty too.

Grange Bridge Cottage Tea Shop
Grange in Borrowdale,
Borrowdale CA12 5UQ
Tel: 01768 777201
Just a few yards from the famous double bridges, this 400-year-old cottage is home to a favourite on the Borrowdale teashop trail. Home-baked cakes, cream teas and light lunches are served in the beautiful Riverside Tea Garden.

The Old Sawmill Tearooms
Mirehouse, Underskiddaw,
Keswick CA12 4QE
Tel: 01768 774317
At the foot of Dodd, just off the A591 and handy for both Mirehouse and the Osprey observation points in Dodd Wood, this lovely woodland tea room serves hot and cold snacks, as well as home-made cakes and scones.

Pubs

Coledale Inn
Braithwaite,
Keswick CA12 5TN
Tel: 01768 778272
www.coledale-inn.co.uk
A large building that has in turn been a woollen mill and a pencil factory. Now it houses a popular walkers' pub. Fresh fish is a feature of the menu, backed up by beef and lamb dishes and a good selection of local ales.

The Old Crown
Hesket Newmarket
CA7 8JD
Tel: 01697 478288
www.theoldcrownpub.co.uk
A beacon in many respects, despite its slightly dilapidated exterior, the Crown is considered to be at the cutting edge of modern country pubs. This may be because it is co-operatively owned by the locals, or because the separate little brewery at the back produces some of Cumbria's finest ales, or may be that the crack is unfailingly excellent.

King's Head
Thirlspot,
Keswick CA12 4TN
Tel: 01768 772393
www.lakedistrictinns.co.uk
This old coaching inn is surrounded by hill scenery. Inside there is a wide choice of regional beers and a menu that makes extensive use of local ingredients and recipes – Cumberland sausage from Waberthwait, duck confit or Jennings steak and ale pie.

The Swinside Inn
Newlands Valley,
Keswick CA12 5UE
Tel: 01768 778253
www.theswinsideinn.com
Sitting on the far side of Swinside, this old inn has great views of both Causey Pike and Cat Bells. Fresh local ingredients include Borrowdale trout and Swinside chicken. Beers tend to be Scottish and Jennings.

Ullswater, Penrith & Eastern Fells

This is a very varied corner of the Lake District. To the south and west is what you would expect from the area: large expanses of water, such as Haweswater and Ullswater, surrounded by soaring mountains like Helvellyn. Head further east, however, and you move through the rolling green Eden Valley, beyond which stand the rugged Pennine hills. There are market towns and ancient monuments, border towns and castles, stately homes and gardens – and fewer crowds.

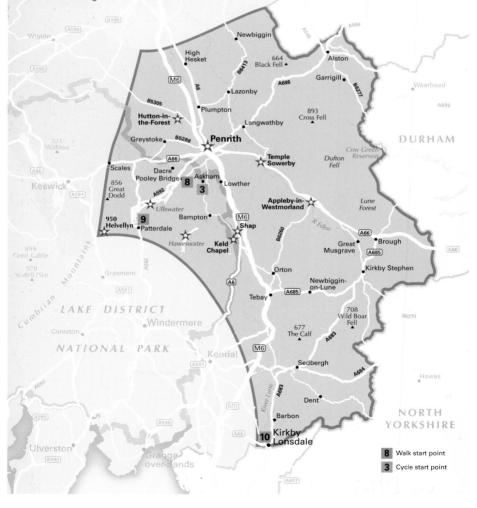

8 Walk start point

3 Cycle start point

HUTTON-IN-THE-FOREST

■ HELVELLYN

Unmissable Attractions

Penrith was the ancient capital of Cumbria. Penrith Beacon on Beacon Hill was lit to warn the inhabitants that border reivers (robbers) raids were imminent but today makes an excellent viewpoint. To the west is Ullswater and Aira Force waterfall. William Wordsworth and Dorothy were walking near here when they spied the 'host of golden daffodils'. The southern tip of the lake below the shoulders of Helvellyn is guarded by the Kirkstone Pass. This was also Wordworth's favourite mountain and is the popular with countless thousands, who trek to its summit. It's a grand climb. Wildlife is abundant in the Haweswater Valley with peregrine falcons, buzzards, sparrowhawks and even golden eagles now breeding in the valley.

1

1 **Ullswater**
Undoubtedly one of the area's loveliest lakes, its waters are exceptionally clear and are surrounded by soaring mountains including Helvellyn.

2 **Appleby**
Situated in Appleby, in the heart of the Elan Valley, parts of sturdy St Lawrence's Church date from the 12th century.

3 **Aira Beck**
A series of splendid waterfalls tumbles down through the lovely wooded gorge of Aira Beck.

4 **Penrith Castle**
Visitors access the striking medieval sandstone remains via a wooden footbridge that spans the castle's moat.

APPLEBY-IN-WESTMORLAND MAP REF NY6820

Appleby has a great deal to commend it, including its setting, in a loop of the tree-lined River Eden, above which its Norman castle stands protectively. Appleby Castle has an impressive 11th-century keep, although a lot of the building dates from the 17th century when it was restored by the redoubtable Lady Anne Clifford. Unfortunately the castle is currently closed to visitors.

Appleby was once the county town of Westmorland, with a royal charter dating from 1174. At either end of its main street, Boroughgate, the High Cross and the Low Cross mark what were the boundaries of Appleby market. The attractive almshouses, known as Lady Anne's Hospital, are still maintained by a trust fund set up by Lady Anne Clifford to provide homes for 13 widows. Lady Anne is buried here in Appleby, her tomb lying in St Lawrence's Church, which can also boast one of the oldest surviving working church organs in the country.

The village of Morland, 7 miles (11.2km) northwest of Appleby, has won several Best Kept Village awards, and the village church has an Anglo-Saxon tower, the oldest in Cumbria.

■ Visit

NENTHEAD

Nenthead Mines Heritage Centre tells the story of how the Quaker London Lead Company left a remarkable social and economic legacy in the north Pennines. The centre, the mines and the village evoke a vivid reminder of past life and work in this remote upland landscape.

HAWESWATER MAP REF NY4713

It may sound like another of nature's lakes, but modern Haweswater is in fact a reservoir, created in the 1930s. Beneath its surface lies the village of Mardale Green and dairy farms of the Haweswater valley. The original lake was much smaller.

However, wildlife abounds in the area, with peregrine falcons, buzzards, sparrowhawks and even golden eagles now breeding in the valley. Otters have also colonised the area, no doubt feeding on the rare char and freshwater herring that are also found here. Other mammals include both roe and red deer, and red squirrels.

On the western shores of the reservoir steep crags rise to the ridge of High Street – high fells taking their name from a Roman road that traverses the summit. In the east is the ancient Naddle Forest, refuge of wood warblers, tree pipits, redstarts and several species of woodpecker. The path which winds through the woods is part of a circular walk around Haweswater and one of the best circular walks in the Lake District.

HELVELLYN MAP REF NY341

Wordsworth's favourite mountain is the favourite of thousands more, who regularly trek to its summit at 3,116 feet (949m). It is a grand climb, but its popularity should not mask its difficulty, as it has arduous stretches, especially on its jagged eastern edges. If you're thinking of venturing on to the hill, make sure you're prepared for sudden changes in weather. Snowfall is not unknown on the tops even as late as

June, and dense mist can envelop them at any time. If you're a novice, try joining one of the many organised groups.

Warnings aside, the peak is accessible by reasonably fit walkers, a popular approach being from Wythburn on the southeastern shores of Thirlmere reservoir. This takes the walker up Helvellyn's steep southwestern slopes, with splendid views across Thirlmere to the west. The eastern approaches are longer but scenically more dramatic, from Grisedale or Glenridding, for example, but you'll need a detailed map.

The arduous climb may have taken your breath away, but the views from the top of Helvellyn will do so again – north along the valley towards Keswick, and east beyond the mountain lake, Red Tarn, to the distant high peaks of the Pennines. Just south of the summit is a memorial by Wordsworth and Sir Walter Scott. The words are a sign that you have reached the highest point in the area. Only Scafell Pike, at 3,210 feet (978m), and Scafell, at 3162 feet (964m), are higher than Helvellyn.

HUTTON-IN-THE-FOREST
MAP REF NY4636
Hutton-in-the-Forest, 7 miles (11km) northwest of Penrith has been the stately home of the Vane family since 1600. It was originally owned by the de Huttons on land they were granted in return for caring for the deer reserve, and for holding the king's stirrup whenever he mounted his horse in Carlisle Castle. Some of the older features include a 17th-century gallery and grand hall.

◼ Activity

CONSERVING CUMBRIA
Visitors can help the environment by parking their cars and using the waymarked walks, cycling, taking the local trains, buses, minibus tours, and launches on the lakes. During the summer an open-top bus service operates between Bowness, Windermere, Ambleside and Grasmere. The Coniston Rambler links Windermere, Ambleside, Hawkshead and Coniston and a service from Keswick leaves for Borrowdale and Buttermere. Minibus tours are a popular way of seeing the high passes; their main centres are Windermere and Keswick.

The grounds are worth seeing, and a particular treat is a walled garden dating from from the 1730s and a wildflower meadow. There is also a lake where nature is largely allowed to take its own course.

PENRITH   MAP REF NY5130
Another borders market town that proved vulnerable to Scottish raiders, Penrith was sacked in the 14th century. Penrith Beacon on Beacon Hill at the town's northern edge was lit to warn the inhabitants of impending raids, and today it is a good viewpoint. The ruined red sandstone castle (English Heritage), which stands in Castle Park, dates from the early 15th century.

There are many more buildings of architectural and historical interest, including Penrith Museum and St Andrew's Church; its graveyard contains the reputed grave of Caesarius, the giant 10th-century Cumbrian king.

Just 1 mile (1.6km) south of Penrith at Eamont Bridge stands Mayburgh Henge. Dating from prehistoric times, its 15-foot (4.5m) banks surround an area of 1.5 acres (0.6ha), inside which is a huge and solitary stone. Close by, King Arthur's Round Table is another ancient henge monument.

Wetheriggs Pottery, 4 miles (6.4km) south of Penrith, has been here since 1855 and the steam-powered pottery site can still be seen. When the pottery closed, its buildings were converted into an animal sanctuary.

Rheged Discovery Centre on the A66, interprets the history of the area through film and a range of innovative techniques. It has some useful shops, play areas and a café.

SHAP & KELD MAP REF NY5615

Shap stone has been used in the making of many fine monuments but the village's own monument is Shap Abbey, by the River Lowther. It was founded in 1199 by the Premonstratensian Order also known as the White Canons from the colour of their habits. The west tower is the most imposing part of the remains, and dates from about 1500. After the Dissolution of the Monasteries, part of the area here was used as a quarry, but the Abbey remains are now safe in the hands of English Heritage.

The National Trust looks after the 15th-century Keld Chapel, in the hamlet of Keld. The simple chapel is still used for occasional services, but is normally locked, though instructions for obtaining the key are pinned to the chapel door.

TEMPLE SOWERBY
MAP REF NY6127

For those who want to see and be inspired by a true host of golden daffodils in the Lake District, then you will find one of the finest spring displays is at Acorn Bank Garden, Temple Sowerby. Whole swathes of yellow bob in the wind beneath the grand oak trees that form an important part of these 2.5 acres (1ha), owned by the National Trust. Acorn Bank is particularly noted for its walled herb garden, which contains the largest collection of medicinal, culinary and even narcotic herbs in the north of England; in all some 250 species. Some are poisonous, so you are warned not to try nibbling them! There are traditional orchards, too, and fine collections of roses, shrubs and herbaceous borders. Gardeners can stock up with plants from the small shop.

The garden is not just of interest to gardeners, though. A circular woodland walk has been created, which makes for a pleasant stroll as it takes the visitor for part of the way through woods alongside Crowdundle Beck and to the restored watermill.

It is the gardens here that originally provided the name for the nearby village of Temple Sowerby, located between Penrith and Appleby. It is known that as long ago as 1228 the Knights Templar had a religious house on this spot, but the oldest parts of the present buildings date back to the 16th century. Nor is the herb garden an ancient one, it was begun by the National Trust who took over care of the gardens in 1969.

Across Heughscar Hill's Roman Road

This is a relatively gentle and straightforward walk, traversing green turf, bracken and white limestone pavement. It offers extensive views west over Ullswater, north across Pooley Bridge and east to the agricultural plain of the Eden Valley. Features of the walk include attractive Pooley Bridge and crossing the High Street Roman road.

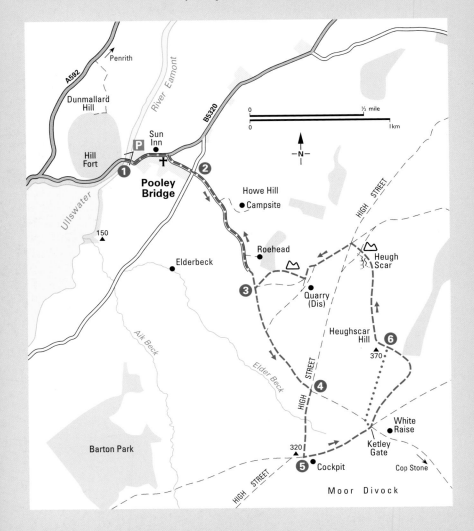

Route Directions

1 From the stone arched bridge crossing the River Eamont follow the main street (B5320) through the centre of Pooley Bridge. Walk on past the church then turn right to follow the pavement along Howtown Road.

2 At the junction continue over the crossroads. The road rises and becomes pleasantly tree-lined before ending at an unsurfaced track beneath Roehead. A pair of gates lead on to the open moor.

3 Go through one of the gates and climb the wide track, continuing to where the going levels and the track crosses the High Street Roman road.

4 Bear right along the resurfaced stretch of Roman road to reach a low circular ancient wall of earth and stone. This, the Cockpit, is the largest of the prehistoric antiquities on Moor Divock.

5 A way leads back diagonally north by the shallow shake holes (sinkholes) to the original track at Ketley Gate. (A little to the right, White Raise burial cairn is worthy of attention.) Either follow the track (the route marked on the map), which leads off northeast ascending to a walled wood high on the hillside and then bear left to find the top of Heughscar Hill, or go left up a well-worn path through the bracken, starting by the stone parish boundary marker. The flat summit of the hill occupies a commanding position offering rewarding views.

6 Proceed north along the high shoulder to pass the broken little limestone crag of Heugh Scar below to the left. At the end of the scar make a steep descent of the grassy hillside crossing a track and continuing down to the point where another track and the grassy lane of the High Street Roman road cross each other. Descend to the left taking the track which passes below the Roman road and head in the general direction of Ullswater. Note a lime kiln and little quarry to the left. Continue the descent to the corner of a stone wall marked by a large sycamore tree. Follow the route which falls steeply down beside the stone wall. Bear left near the bottom of the incline and gain the original broad track just above the gates near Roehead. Return by the same road back to Pooley Bridge.

Route facts

DISTANCE/TIME
4.5 miles (7.2km) 2hr

MAP OS Explorer OL5 The English Lakes (NE)

START Pay car parks either side of bridge; grid ref: NY 470244

TRACKS Village, dale and open fell

GETTING TO THE START
Pooley Bridge is at the foot of Ullswater and can be approached on the A592 from Penrith or the B5320 from Eamont Bridge. The walk begins from the car park on the western side of the bridge, but there are other parking areas in the village.

THE PUB
The Sun Inn, Pooley Bridge, see Point 1 on route. Tel: 017684 86205 www.suninnpooleybridge. co.uk

❶ Surfaced roads, stony tracks, grassy tracks and hillside

From Patterdale by Ullswater

Ullswater is undoubtedly one of the loveliest lakes. It was the sight of golden daffodils among the trees and beside the shore that inspired William Wordsworth's most widely known poem, 'I wandered lonely as a cloud' (1807). This walk takes you along the shores of Ullswater to Silver Point, a spectacular viewpoint.

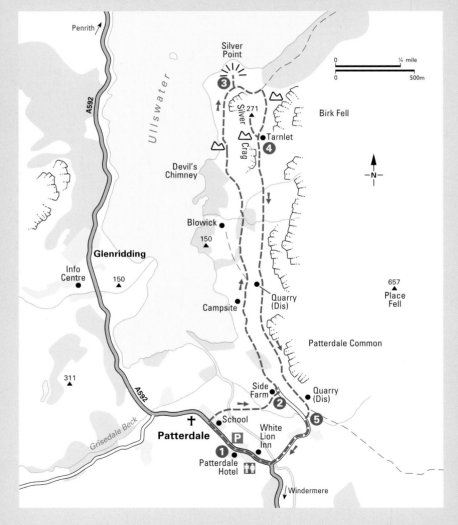

Route Directions

1 From the car park walk to the road and turn right towards the shore of Ullswater. Pass the school to a track leading off right, through the buildings. Follow the unsurfaced track which takes you over a bridge and continue through the buildings of Side Farm to join another unsurfaced track.

2 Turn left along the undulating track, with a stone wall to the left, and pass through mixed woodland, predominantly oak and ash, before open fellside appears above. Proceed along the path above the campsite and pass a stand of larch before descending to cross a little stream above the buildings of Blowick, seen through the trees below. The path ascends again to crest a craggy knoll above the woods of Devil's Chimney. Make a steep descent following the path through the rocks before it levels to traverse beneath the craggy heights of Silver Crag. A slight ascent, passing some fine holly trees, gains the shoulder of Silver Point and an outstanding view of Ullswater. A short there-and-back to the tip is worthwhile.

3 Follow the path, which sweeps beneath the end of Silver Crag and continue to pass a small stream before a steep stony path, eroded in places, breaks off to the right. Ascend this, climbing diagonally right, through the juniper bushes. Gain the narrow gap which separates Silver Crag to the right from the main hillside of Birk Fell to the left. This little valley is quite boggy and holds a small tarnlet.

4 If you don't care for steep, exposed ground, follow the high narrow path to make a gradual descent south in the direction of Patterdale. But for those with a head for heights, a short steep scramble leads to the top of Silver Crag and a wonderful view. Care must be exercised for steep ground lies in all directions. Descend back to the ravine and the main path by the same route. The path is easy though it traverses the open fellside and may be boggy in places. Pass open quarry workings, where there is a large unfenced hole next to the path (take care), and continue on, to cross over the slate scree of a larger quarry. Bear right to descend by a stream and cross a little footbridge leading to the gate at the end of a track.

5 Go left through the gate and follow the lane which leads through the meadows. Cross the bridge and join the road. Bear right through Patterdale to return to the car park.

Route facts

DISTANCE/TIME
4 miles (6.4km)1h45

MAP OS Explorer OL5 The English Lakes (NE)

START Pay-and-display car park, Patterdale; grid ref: NY 396159

TRACKS Stony tracks and paths, no stiles

GETTING TO THE START
Patterdale village lies at the southern tip of Ullswater, stretched along the A592. The car park is opposite the Patterdale Hotel.

THE PUB White Lion, Patterdale, at the end of the walk.
Tel: 017684 82214

❶ Rough tracks with some steep sections. Suitability: children 8+

ULLSWATER MAP REF NY4220

On the western shores of Ullswater, a series of splendid waterfalls tumbles down through the wooded gorge of Aira Beck which flows into the region's second largest lake, some 7.5 miles (12km) long. The falls are known by the name of the largest, the 70-foot (21.3m) drop of Aira Force, on land owned by the National Trust. There's also an arboretum, a café and a landscaped Victorian park.

Back in 1802, the falls didn't just feed the waters of Ullswater, they fed the imagination of William and Dorothy Wordsworth. The poet and his sister were walking near by, when Dorothy observed the 'daffodils so beautiful... they tossed and reeled and danced.' Her words were transformed into one of the best-known and best-loved of English poems, William Wordsworth's Daffodils. Aira Force itself is also the setting for another of William Wordsworth's poems, *The Somnambulist*.

It is appropriate that the poet was inspired by what, for many people, is the lake among lakes, indisputably beautiful. The southern tip of its slim shape is below the shoulders of Helvellyn, to the west, and is reached through the dramatic and high Kirkstone Pass, which rises to 1,489 feet (454m). Near here is the Kirkstone Pass Inn, third highest pub in the country. Look, too, for the rock which is said to resemble a church steeple and which gives the pass its name – church-stone.

At Pooley Bridge on the lake's northern tip, a fish market used to be held in the main square, and this area is still rich in trout and salmon. A short walk up to Dunmallard Hill reveals Iron Age remains. Below here at the pier near the 16th-century bridge, two 19th-century steamers leave to take visitors down the lake. The two ships, *Lady of the Lake* and *Raven*, date from 1877 and 1889 respectively, an indication of how long visitors have been enjoying these waters.

The steamers (diesel-powered since the 1930s) call at Howtown, roughly halfway along Ullswater's eastern shore, then travel on to Glenridding at the southern end. A popular option is to combine a cruise with a walk, and no finer walk is said to exist in the Lakes than that between Howtown and Glenridding. For much of the way the footpath, rough in places, skirts Ullswater's shores, with magnificent views across the waters and Helvellyn rising beyond. There is no road through this steep-cliffed southeastern shore of the lake. The cruise boat can then be rejoined at Glenridding, but don't let the distances deceive you. The lake may be only 7.5 miles (12km) long, but that is also roughly the distance by foot from Howtown to Glenridding. The curve of its crescent shape here accounts for the rest, with an extra stretch round the bottom loop of the lake.

Near Howtown the lake narrows to about 400 yards (366m) at the strangely named Skelly Nab. The name derives from the freshwater herring, the schelly, found only here, in Haweswater and high up in the Red Tarn on Helvellyn. The silvery foot-long fish were once caught in nets strung between Skelly Nab and the opposite shore.

Around Askham and Bampton

This pleasant road circuit has few steep gradients and is away from the main tourist routes. It is rich in ancient hedgerows and is a great ride for wildflower-spotting.

Route Directions

1 From the car park follow the main road south through the village, dog-legging past the Queens Head pub, with the greens stretching off to left and right. Keep on along this road, enjoying the generally easy gradients and views down the valley to the Shap Fells. Across the valley on the left is the sharp profile of Knipe Scar.

2 After just over 1 mile (1.6km), on the boundary of Helton, branch off right on a loop road to go through the village. The extra climb is worth it for the pretty cottages and flowery verges. Ease back to rejoin the valley road and continue, with limestone walls and small fields flanking the road on the right. As the road starts to descend, two lanes branch off to the right from a shared junction.

3 Follow the left-hand lane for 400yds (366m) to a cattle grid, for a look at the old mill, with an overgrown watercourse, on Heltondale Beck. Continue a little further until the lane reaches open

fell. There are good views here and you may find fell ponies grazing. Retrace to the road at the start of Point 3 and turn right to continue, now descending. At the bottom swing right over Beckfoot Bridge and continue along the level valley floor, passing more pretty cottages at Butterwick. The walls here have changed from silvery limestone to greyer Lakeland rock. Climb a little to the outskirts of Bampton, then go down into the village.

4 The post office and village shop has a café attached, information panels on the wall and more inside. Over the bridge opposite the shop, it's just a short way up the lane to the pretty Mardale Inn. (For a longer ride continue up this lane for 2 miles/3.2km to Naddle Bridge and Haweswater.) Continue along the main valley road towards Bampton Grange, swinging left into the village over a bridge crossing the River Lowther, and past the Crown and Mitre pub.

Route facts

DISTANCE/TIME 8.75 miles (14.2km) 1h

MAP OS Explorer OL5 The English Lakes (NE)

START Village car park, Askham; grid ref: NY 513237

TRACKS Quiet lanes

GETTING TO THE START
Askham is south of Penrith and the M6, junction 40. From there, take the A66 east. Turn right on the A6, go through Eamont Bridge, then turn right on the B5320. Go over a railway bridge, then turn left to reach Askham. There is a signposted car park on the left as you enter the village.

THE PUB Queens Head, Askham, see Point 1 on route. Tel: 01931 712225

❶ Few steep climbs and descents. Suitability: children 8+

5 On the edge of the village, turn left, signposted 'Knipe, Whale'. Look back to the left over Bampton Grange, with the fells behind rising to the great smooth ridges where the Romans built a road now known as High Street. Cross a cattle grid on to open fell. Look up to the right to the low crags of Knipe Scar. The lane climbs gently, with great views of the valley and the fells to the west. Descend

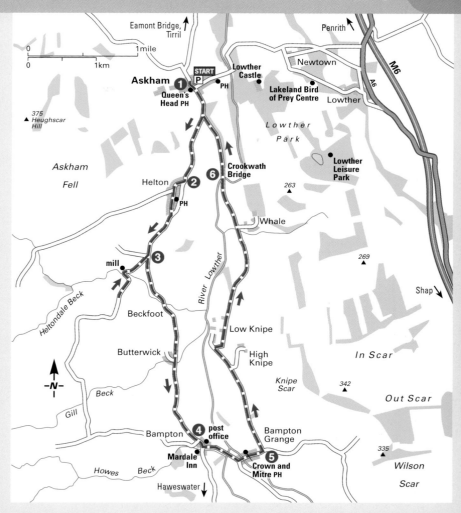

to a junction by a phone box and turn right through a gate. Climb steeply to another gate, beyond which the road continues to climb gradually. The going levels off for a stretch before beginning to descend. Whizz back down into the valley, keeping straight on at a junction, and down to the river at Crookwath Bridge.

6 The climb away from the river is gentle but quite sustained. It then levels off just before a T-junction. Emerge with care as some traffic moves quite fast here, and almost immediately go right, back into Askham.

Kirkby Lonsdale to Whittington

From the old market town to Whittington village, on the Cumbria/Lancashire border.
This circular walk goes over rolling hills, through farmland and woods, to the worthy
village of Whittington then to return along the banks of the lovely Lune. The walk
passes close to Sellet Mill, reputedly the second largest waterwheel in Britain.

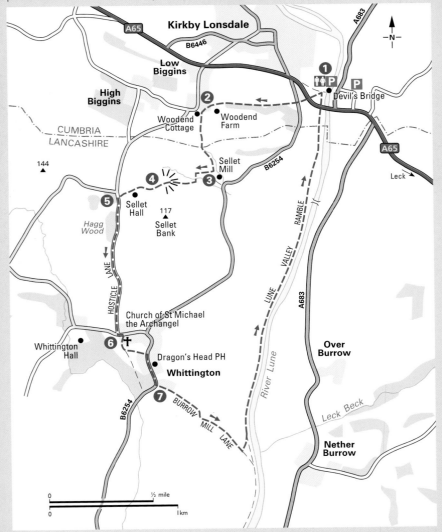

Route Directions

1 From the west bank of the river, a few paces downstream from Devil's Bridge, go diagonally up across a park with picnic tables to a kissing gate near paired conifers. Cross the A65, go through a narrow meadow and between houses and cross the B6254. Enter another meadow, go uphill, keeping the walled wooded area on your left. Yellow markers help you find the route. Keep on over the brow of the hill and straight ahead through two kissing gates to a metal gate near houses. Bear left to a signpost.

2 Cross a farm track and walk in front of white-painted Woodend Cottage to enter a walled path (rough in places). Lower down, a stream comes (left) and tries to take over the path; escape rightwards to drier ground before the millpond of Sellet Mill. Go past sheds to a farmyard.

3 Turn right over a stile, walk up the field, keeping the fence to your left, until just past the end of a garden. Go left through a yellow marked gate and walk straight across a small field to another marked gate followed immediately by a shallow stream. Turn right to go round Sellet Bank, aiming initially for the corner of a hedge under power-lines. Continue with hedge to your right. Look back for views of Leck Fell and Barbon Fell.

4 As the hedge bears left, cross it through a yellow marked stile, right. Skirt round a wooded area. Facing Sellet Hall, turn right adjacent to fenced driveway following marker arrows. Keep on over the corner of the field, cross a stile and drop down to the road at a T-junction. Turn left along Hosticle Lane towards Whittington.

5 The lane, sunken in places, carries very little traffic. It steepens as you approach the outskirts of Whittington.

6 Go left at the T-junction for a few paces, cross the road and turn right over a pebbled mosaic at the entrance to the Church of St Michael the Archangel. Keep the square bell tower on your left, descend stone steps to go through a narrow stile and the modern graveyard. Follow the hedge to a gate in the left corner and keep straight on to a stone stile into a walled path leading to Main Street. Turn right, walk through the village past the village hall and the Dragon's Head pub.

Route facts

DISTANCE/TIME 4.75 miles (7.7km) 2h30

MAP OS Explorer OL2 Yorkshire Dales – Southern & Western

START Devil's Bridge car park, Kirkby Lonsdale; grid ref: SD 615782

TRACKS Overgrown and indistinct in patches, quiet lanes and tracks, 17 stiles

GETTING TO THE START Turn north off the A65 on the A683, cross the bridge, and then take the next, sharp, right turn to the car park.

THE PUB Dragon's Head, Whittington, see Point 6 on route. Tel: 015242 72383

❶ Very rough path after Wood End Farm. Suitability: children 6+

7 At a sharp right bend on the village edge, turn left along a gritty track. Pass a farm and tennis courts. Continue between fields. Cross a cattle grid, reach a hut beside the Lune. Follow 'Lune Valley Ramble' upstream. There's a short overgrown section but it soon becomes an easy walk through fields, close to the river. The route is obvious back to the A65 bridge at Kirkby Lonsdale. Go through a gate and up steps to the left of the parapet. Cross the road and descend to cross the park at the start of the walk.

■ TOURIST INFORMATION CENTRES

Alston
Town Hall, Front Street.
Tel: 01434 382244

Appleby-in Westmorland
Moot Hall, Boroughgate.
Tel: 01768 351177

Kirkby Stephen
Market Street.
Tel: 01768 371199

Penrith
Robinson's School,
Middlegate.
Tel: 0176 8867466

Southwaite
M6 Service Area.
Tel: 01697 473445/6

Rheged Discovery Centre
Redhills, Penrith.
Tel: 01768 860034

Ullswater
Main Car Park, Glenridding.
Tel: 01768 482414

■ PLACES OF INTEREST

Acorn Bank Garden
Temple Sowerby.
Tel: 01768 361893.
Delightful garden by
Crowdundle Beck.

Brougham Castle
Brougham.
Tel: 01768 862488.
Impressive 13th-century
remains on the banks of the
River Eamont. Southeast
of Penrith.

Brough Castle
Church Brough, Brough.
Tel: 0870 333 1181

Massive Norman ruins on a
Roman foundation guarding
Stainmore Pass.

Brougham Hall
Brougham.
Tel: 01768 868184.
Craft centre and museum
in a 15th-century ruin.

Dalemain
Pooley Bridge, Dacre.
Tel: 01768 486450
Delightful country house
with gardens and parkland.

Hutton-in-the-Forest
Skelton. Tel: 01768 484449

Little Salkeld Watermill
Little Salkeld, Penrith.
Tel: 01768 881523. Free.

Long Meg Stone Circle
Little Salkeld, Penrith. Free.

**Nenthead Mines
Heritage Centre**
Nenthead, Alston.
Tel: 01434 382037

Penrith Castle
Opposite Penrith railway
station. Free.

Penrith Museum
Robinson's School, Penrith.
Tel: 01768 212228

Rheged Discovery Centre
Redhills, Penrith.
Tel: 01768 868000;
www.rheged.com.
Exhibitions, restaurant, coffee
shop and shops.

Shap Abbey
Shap. Premonstratensian
abbey moved from Preston
Patrick to Shap c1199.
Free.

South Tynedale Railway
The Railway Station,
Hexham Road, Alston.
Tel: 01434 381696

■ FOR CHILDREN

Eden Ostrich World
Langwathby.
Tel: 01768 881771;
www.ostrich-world.com
Ostriches and other animals.
Indoor soft play area.

**Lakeland Bird
of Prey Centre**
Old Walled Garden, Lowther.
Tel: 01931 712746
Flying demonstrations.

■ SHOPPING

Appleby-in-Westmorland
Open-air market, Sat.

Penrith
Open-air market, Tue. Sat.
at Auction Mart.

LOCAL SPECIALITIES

Cumberland Sausage
Butchers around Penrith.
Several supply J & J Graham,
Market Place, Penrith.
Cranstons Cumbrian Food
Hall, Ullswater Road,
Penrith.
Tel: 01768 868680

Cheese
Smoked Cumberland cheese
and other specialities can be
found at Taste@Rheged.

Crafts
Gossipgate Gallery,
The Butts, Alston.
Tel: 01434 381806

The Rheged Shop, Rheged Discovery Centre, Redhills, Penrith. Tel: 01768 868000; www.rheged.com
Upfront Gallery, Unthank, Skelton, Penrith. Tel: 01768 484538

Mustard

Cumberland mustard is sold in Alston, Taste@Rheged and several other places in the Eden Valley.

■ **OUTDOOR ACTIVITIES**

ANGLING

River Eden,

Haweswater & Ullswater

Permits are required, visit www.edenrivertrust.org.uk or contact the local TICs. Bessy Beck Trout Fishery, Newbiggin-on-Lune, near Kirkby Stephen. Tel: 01539 623303
Blencarn Lake, near Penrith. Tel: 01768 88284

BOAT TRIPS

Ullswater

Ullswater Steamers. Tel: 01768 482229

CYCLE HIRE

Glenridding

St Patrick's Boat Centre. Tel: 01768 482393

Penrith

Arragon's Cycle Centre, Brunswick Road. Tel: 01768 890344

Pooley Bridge

Park Foot Caravan Site. Tel: 01768 486309

GUIDED WALKS

Settle–Carlisle Railway

Guided walks from several stations in the Eden Valley. www.settle-carlisle.co.uk

HORSE-RIDING

Little Salkeld

Bank House Equestrian. Tel: 01768 881257

Troutbeck, Penrith

Rookin House Farm. Tel: 01768 483561

LONG-DISTANCE FOOTPATHS AND TRAILS

The Pennine Way

The country's premier National Trail traverses the high Pennine ridge between Dufton and Alston.

Coast-to-Coast Walk

A 190-mile (304km) walk from St Bees Head to Robin Hood's Bay, North Yorkshire.

SAILING

Glenridding

Sailing Centre, The Spit. Tel: 01768 482541

■ **ANNUAL EVENTS & CUSTOMS**

Alston

Alston Sheepdog Trials, Jun. Alston Gala Day, early Jul. Alston and District Flower Show, early Sep.

Appleby-in-Westmorland

Appleby New Fair (Horse Fair), second week Jun. Appleby Town Carnival and Sports, mid-Jul. Jazz Festival, Jun.

Appleby Agricultural Show, early Aug.
Appleby and District Gardeners' Society Show, early Sep.

Bampton

Bampton Sports Day, Jun.

Musgrave

Musgrave Rushbearing, Jul.

Patterdale

Patterdale sheepdog trials, end Aug.

Penrith

Cumbria Fell and Dales Pony Show, May
Agricultural Show, late Jul.
Potfest, end of Jul.
Lakeland Fell Pony Show, early Aug.

Shap

Shap Sheepdog Trials, Jun.

Skelton

Skelton Show, mid-Aug.

Warcop

Warcop Rushbearing, Jun.

Tea Rooms

Acorn Bank
**Temple Sowerby,
Penrith CA10 1SP
Tel: 01768 361893;
www.nationaltrust.org**

A visit to Acorn Bank's tea room is the only chance you'll get to see inside this 17th-century mansion. The National Trust tradition of excellent home-made cakes continues here alongside Fairtrade teas and coffees. Lunches and a children's menu are also available.

Fellbites Café
**Glenridding,
Penrith CA11 0PD
Tel: 01768 482664**

At the centre of Glenridding, by the main car parks, Fellbites couldn't be more conveniently placed for visitors to this beautiful valley. Ullswater trout is a favourite on the lunch menu, or you could try one of the many Lakeland-recipe cakes.

The Watermill Tearoom
**Little Salkeld,
Penrith CA10 1NN
Tel: 01768 881523;
www.organicmill.co.uk**

This little café is attached to the watermill itself. It sells its organic flour and other goodies and has a classroom for various breadmaking courses. The Gallery displays local crafts. After tasting the wholesome vegetarian fare, you can pop next door and watch the flour being milled.

Greystone House Farm Shop and Tearoom
**Stainton, Penrith CA11 0EF
Tel: 01768 866952**

The oak-beamed lofthouse tea room is a great place to sample some of the locally sourced ingredients sold in the shop. Lunches, snacks, home-baked scones and cakes are all freshly prepared and a speciality is the farm's own beef and lamb.

Pubs

Black Swan
**Ravenstonedale, near Kirkby Stephen CA17 4NG
Tel: 01539 623204**

Good food, real ales and a friendly welcome are only part of the story of this fine Victorian hotel which also houses the village shop. Local lamb and fish are highlights of a changing menu, which also includes lighter refreshments.

George and Dragon
**Clifton, Penrith CA10 2ER
Tel: 01768 865381**

Taking much of its food from the Lowther Estate, this wayside inn just outside Penrith has become a notable success for the Lowther family, whose presence in the area as Earls of Lonsdale is measured in centuries. There's plenty to choose from, whether it's venison, lamb, mutton, pork or beef. The beer is local too.

Highland Drove
**Great Salkeld, Penrith CA11 9NA
Tel: 01768 898349**

The upstairs Kyloes restaurant takes its name from the cattle that would be driven this way from Scotland to market in England during the 18th and 19th centuries. It caters to a more formal dining taste, though retains a friendly, down to earth atmosphere. Downstairs this is a comfortable village pub, with good beer and a loyal local following as well as being popular with visitors.

Traveller's Rest
**Greenside Road, Glenridding, Penrith CA11 0QQ
Tel: 01768 482298**

There is no better place to unwind after climbing Helvellyn than in this cosy pub halfway up the road to Greenside mine. Stay for a generous home-cooked meal, or sit outside with a pint and watch the walkers.

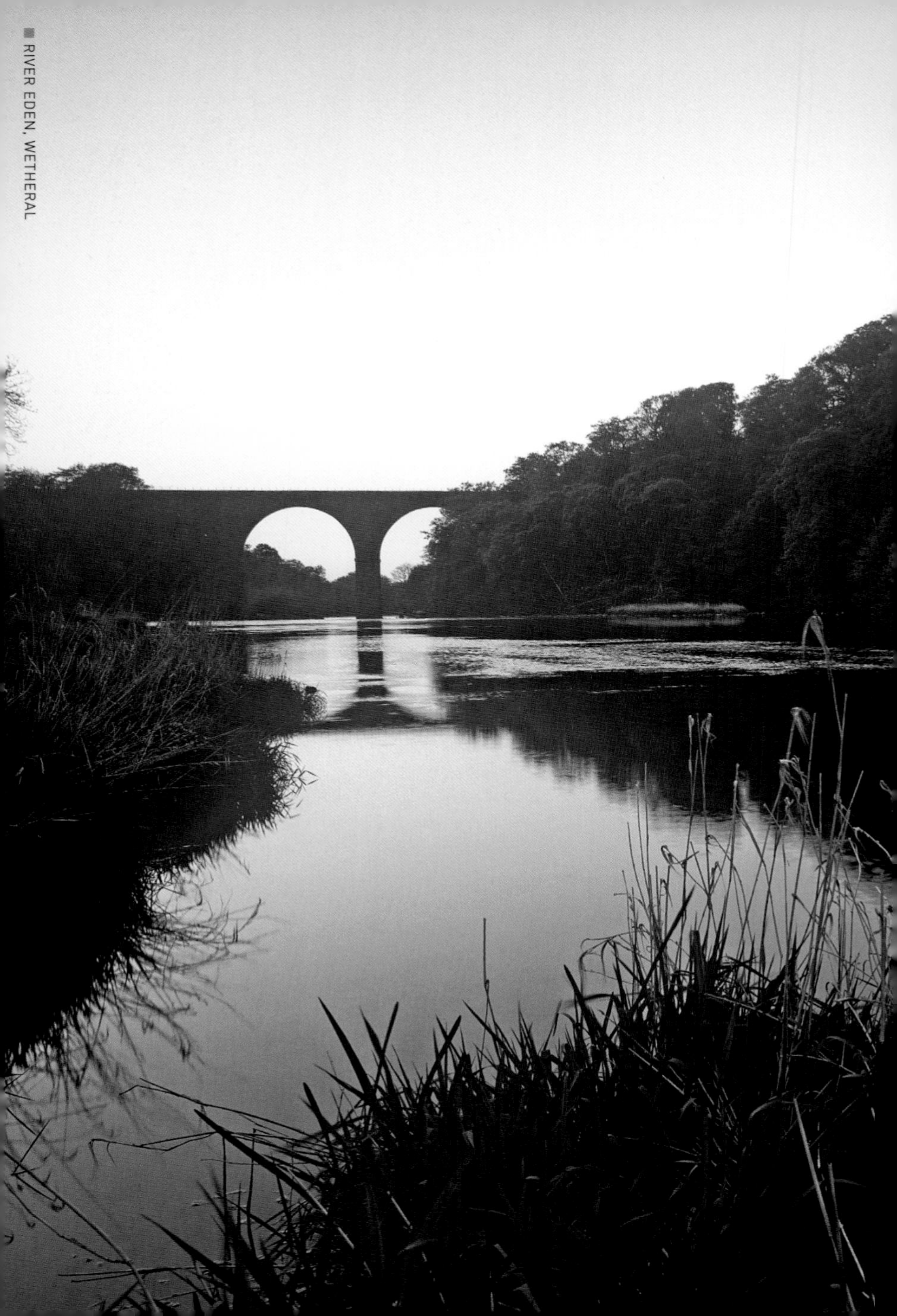

RIVER EDEN, WETHERAL

Carlisle & Borderlands

This fascinating corner of England is often neglected by guidebooks. Yet Carlisle is only 20 miles (32km) from Keswick for that famous flying crow, if twice the distance in a dog-leg drive. It is a land for those with an interest in its dramatic and often romantic history, for this is a land of reivers, of 'Bonnie' Prince Charlie, of castles and priories, of the Romans and Hadrian's Wall. If its low-lying landscape means less visual drama, there is certainly no lack of the historical kind, with Carlisle's museums, old buildings, castle and cathedral as its focus.

2 Tour start point

BIRDOSWALD

LANERCOST PRIORY

Unmissable attractions

Visitors to the Lake District often miss out the northernmost point of Cumbria but on the remote border between England and Scotland, where warfare was endemic until the mid-18th century, this beautiful landscape and its sparse settlements bear the marks of continual violence. Most striking of all is Hadrian's Wall, 73 miles (117.5km) long and almost 2,000 years old, marking the northern boundary of the Roman Empire. Carlisle Castle and city walls were begun by William Rufus, who recaptured it from the Scots in 1092. In the surrounding towns and villages you'll find an area rich in historical associations and remains.

1 Lanercost Priory
Set amid meadows between the River Irthing and Hadrian's Wall, this medieval monastic site retains many fine elements including the parish church.

2 Hadrian's Wall
The World Heritage Site of Hadrian's Wall marked the northern limits of the Roman Empire and can be traced both in stone and as a series of ditches, roads, forts and settlements.

3 Arthuret Church, Longtown
Arthuret Church on the outskirts of Longtown, dates from 1150, but the present Church was built in 1609 in late Gothic style. Archie Armstrong, favourite Court Jester to James I, and later Charles I, is buried in the Churchyard.

4 Bewcastle castle ruins
The medieval castle at Bewcastle is just one feature of a historic site which includes a Roman fort and a superb Saxon-era cross.

5 Carlisle
Carlisle's huge castle saw action as late as 1745, and is linked by the Millennium Walkway to the city's Tullie House Museum and Art Gallery.

BEWCASTLE   MAP REF NY5674

In the churchyard of this remote corner of Cumbria, 3 miles (4.8km) east of the B6318 and less than 7 miles (11.2km) from the Scottish border, stands Bewcastle Cross, one of the oldest and finest stone crosses in Europe. It is a cross without its cross, however, as the top fell off and no one knows what happened to it. Still a magnificent sight, however, it stands over 13 feet (4m) high and is made of yellow sandstone. Its weathered surface is patterned with early Celtic scrolls and intricate designs, and decorated with carvings first made some 1,300 years ago.

Just to the south is Hadrian's Wall, and the castle at Bewcastle – now ruined – was built in about 1092 on the site of a former Roman fort. The castle's south wall is still standing, to almost its full height, but it is a castle to be appreciated for its setting rather than its state of preservation.

A nearby village pub, the Drove, carries echoes of the one-time drovers' roads, which passed by here. A former inn, near by, was named the Lime Kiln after the lime industry which flourished here. Some old kilns can still be seen in the surrounding countryside, and on the border with Scotland, the remote Bailey district has several limestone quarries hidden amongst its craggy hills.

BIRDOSWALD   MAP REF NY6266

Above the dramatic Irthing Gorge, with a picnic area now looking out over it, the remote 5-acre (2ha) remains of the Roman fort and settlement at Birdoswald is the most interesting spot in this western expanse of Hadrian's Wall. It was built in about AD 125 when its Roman name was Banna, and at its busiest would have housed up to 500 foot soldiers. They were there to protect this length of wall, and in particular their bridge across the River Irthing, from the Scots. Although the Wall itself is lower here than it is further east, the part of it that runs eastwards from Birdoswald towards Harrow's Scar is the longest visible remaining stretch – a strong reminder of its original scale.

Of the fort itself, mainly the perimeter wall remains, with its entrance gates and part of one turret. Nevertheless, with the help of an interactive visitor centre, a vivid picture emerges of Birdoswald in Roman times. Excavations have unearthed the granaries, added in about AD 200, and other finds have included an 'Arm Purse' containing 28 silver coins, and some delicate gold jewellery now on display in Carlisle's Tullie House Museum. A visit here is certainly recommended after seeing the site itself.

■ Visit

TURF WORK

From Harrow's Scar near Birdoswald to its end at the Solway Firth, a distance of 30 miles (48km), Hadrian's Wall was originally made of turf. Its rebuilding in stone took place partly during Hadrian's reign, and partly from AD 160. A 2-mile (3.2km) stretch of the wall west of the River Irthing did not follow the line of the original wall, so some of the remains of the turf wall can still be seen running near by. Some of the turrets are free-standing, to enable turf ramparts to be run up them.

BRAMPTON MAP REF NY5316

One of Cumbria's many small and attractive market towns, Brampton has held its charter since 1252. The cobbled square around the Moot Hall bustles each Wednesday, although not as much as it would have done in 1745, when Brampton was the headquarters of Bonnie Prince Charlie's army while it was laying siege to Carlisle Castle. Seek out St Martin's Church, which has stained-glass windows by William Morris and Edward Burne-Jones.

The Augustinian Priory at Lanercost, in a wooded valley 2 miles (3.2km) northeast of Brampton, was dedicated to St Mary Magdalene in 1169. Although much of it is in ruins, including the main priory buildings, the nave of the church still survives and has been used as the parish church from the mid-1700s to the present day. Its vaulted ceilings are splendid. Unfortunately its location, close to the Scottish border, made it the subject of Scottish raids over the centuries, hastening its downfall.

CARLISLE MAP REF NY3956

If you want to begin with the history of Carlisle, then a visit to the award-winning Tullie House Museum and Art Gallery in Castle Street with its interactive displays, is the place to start. It traces the history of Carlisle from before the Romans to the railways and beyond, via the reivers, Robert the Bruce and the Roundheads. It also has very good natural history displays. A great deal of thought has gone into the exhibits, which combine education and entertainment. You can try writing on

■ Insight

WILLIAM WALLACE

William 'Braveheart' Wallace, who is known to have raided Lanercost Priory, was born in about the year 1274. He was an early campaigner for Scottish independence from the English, who ruled the country at the time. He was a man who believed in action, too. In 1297 he killed the English sheriff in Lanark, and went on to defeat Edward I's army at Stirling Bridge before moving into northern England. By 1298, however, Edward I's troops had begun to fight back and defeated Wallace at Falkirk. After escaping to France he returned to Scotland but was arrested in 1305. That same year he was hanged, drawn and quartered in London, the quarters of his body being sent to Newcastle, Berwick, Stirling and Perth.

Roman wax tablets, have a go on a crossbow, or go through a mine tunnel.

Linked to the museum by the Millennium Gallery, Carlisle Castle dates from 1092 when the first castle was built by William II. The keep dates from then, but many of the distinctive rounded battlements were added by Henry VIII to house artillery. Several rooms in the gatehouse are decorated in medieval style, while inside the castle a warren of chambers and passageways can be explored. The castle was captured by 'Bonnie' Prince Charlie in 1745, and Mary, Queen of Scots was imprisoned here. Also here is the Museum of the Border Regiment. Its collection of weaponry, uniforms, medals and other items reveal many tragic and heroic stories from the wars in which the regiment has been involved.

In 1122, 30 years after the castle was built, Carlisle Cathedral was founded. It was originally a priory but became a cathedral under Henry I in 1132 and can claim to have held a daily service for almost 900 years. Inside, the first thing to strike the eye is the magnificent high ceiling. Its stained glass dates from the 14th to the 20th centuries – the oldest is in the East Window. Do not miss seeing the buildings opposite the cathedral's main entrance. The Fratry was a 13th-century monastic common room and now contains the cathedral library and the Prior's Kitchen Restaurant. Across from the Fratry, the 13th-century Prior's Tower was used, among other things, as a place of refuge from reivers and other Scottish raiders. Inside the tower, which can be seen by arrangement, is a ceiling with 45 panels, hand-painted in 1510.

Slightly overshadowed by the cathedral, but worth a visit, is St Cuthbert's Church, which was also built in the 12th century, although the present buildings date from the 1700s. Its most unusual feature is a moveable pulpit, mounted on rail tracks, while the nearby tithe barn is now the church hall.

The city walls give some idea of the extent of the place in Roman times, as they were built – some 1,000 years after Hadrian's Wall – around the remains of the Roman town and fort. The West Walls, which run behind St Cuthbert's and around the cathedral, are the best surviving examples. These were begun in 1122 but not completed until 1200.

Carlisle's timber-framed Guildhall was built in 1404 and now houses the Guildhall Museum. Other notable buildings include the Citadel with its 19th-century towers dominating Henry VIII's 16th-century entrance to the city and the 18th-century Town Hall which is now used as a visitor centre.

HADRIAN'S WALL

In about AD 121, the Roman soldiers stationed in what became northern England began to build a wall that was to run for 73 miles (117.5km), from the Solway Firth to the River Tyne. Working under the instructions of the Emperor Hadrian (AD 76–138), the soldiers produced a barrier that would keep out the wild tribes of northern Britain, while Rome tried to civilise those behind the wall by introducing such features as central heating, public baths and an efficient drainage system.

There are several examples of such Roman remains at places along the Wall, though the finest examples – Chesters, Corbridge, Vindolanda and Housesteads – are to the east. In addition to the fort at Birdoswald, some parts of the western section of the Wall are worth visiting. There are the remains of turrets at Piper Sike, Leahill and Banks East, while at Hare Hill, near Lanercost, is a section of the Wall that stands 9 feet (2.7m) high.

The Wall now forms the western part of a UNESCO World Heritage Site – 'The Frontiers of the Roman Empire' – which includes large sections of Wall across Germany. The Hadrian's Wall Path National Trail between Bowness-on-Solway and Tynemouth opened in 2004 and is now one of England's most popular National Trails.

The Reivers' Tour

From the 4th to the late 17th centuries, the land around Carlisle, on the hazy border between England and Scotland was one of the most lawless places in Britain. Reivers were the villainous families who lived on either side of the border and who plundered each other's property and cattle, killing each other into the bargain. There was even a a reiving thieving season, beginning in August and lasting for three months, until the law courts reconvened. Today the quiet, beautiful countryside gives no indication of the hell on earth this area must have been for its inhabitants. Reiving has left its dreadful mark on the English language with the word 'bereaved'.

Route Directions

The length of this tour is 68 miles (109km), it begins at Carlisle, the county town of Cumbria and the largest city in the area. There has been a settlement here since Celtic times, followed by the Romans, the Romano-Celts, Anglo-Saxons, Danes, Normans, Scots and English. Carlisle's imposing castle, which now houses a Regimental Museum, is a reminder of this constant conflict. The cathedral, built by the Normans, is also an indication of their search for peace after creating mayhem in the district, as they did in the rest of Britain. Visit the Reivers Exhibition at Tullie House to gain an accurate picture of the time and events, before starting out on your journey into the past.

1 Leave Carlisle on the A7. Drive round Hardwicke Circus roundabout and cross the River Eden. Shortly go right along the B6264 towards Hexham and Newcastle. This is the area through which cattle, sheep and vegetables were brought to Carlisle. As Carlisle had been the traditional market centre for miles around and as roads were practically non-existent, the people had very little choice in where they could go to get the best prices.

2 Cross the M6 and meet a roundabout, where you take the 2nd exit on to the A689. Pass the airport runway and then turn left with the sign to the airport and Irthington. Continue through Irthington. Here in Irthington village only a grassy mound remains of the Norman castle that once stood here.

3 About a mile (1.6km) after Irthington, turn right on to the A6071 and keep ahead. After crossing the bridge, turn left to Walton.

The course of Hadrian's Wall passes through the village. There was once a fort at Castlesteads, in the trees up to your left as you enter. There is little to see in the way of remains here, but the Wall's National Trail passes through.

4 Keep forward through Walton and at the junction with the B6318 turn right, signposted 'Gilsland and Greenhead'. Just after a mile (1.6km) turn left for Askerton Castle and Bewcastle church. At Bewcastle turn right up to the church and the cross. Bewcastle is very close to the Scottish border and this proximity was one of the reasons that made it the focus for reiving activity – consequntly there were many tracks leading through the area. In 1582 Thomas Musgrave, Captain of Bewcastle, and his tenants lost 700 cattle, 300 sheep, and crops and buildings were burned. The history of Bewcastle goes back much further – to Celtic and Roman times. During the 2nd and 3rd centuries AD there were around 1,000 Roman soldiers stationed here. In the churchyard the Bewcastle Cross is an excellent example of Anglo-Saxon sculpture and a very early Christian memorial, as the majority of Anglo-Saxons were still pagans at this time. During the time of the reivers, it was said that only women were buried in the churchyard, because all the men were hanged in Carlisle.

5 At Bewcastle, turn left. At the junction take the right fork. Go right at the T-junction on to the B6318, which bears left. Continue for 4 miles (6.4km) to where the B6318 turns left. Do not take this left turn but continue straight ahead on a minor road, then bear right at the next junction, heading for Newcastleton. You are now in Scotland. In Newcastleton take the opportunity to visit the Liddesdale Heritage Centre and Museum. This history museum and genealogical research facility houses a large collection of artefacts. A commemorative bi-centenary tapestry created by local needleworkers is a unique

exhibit. The museum also includes a superb collection of railway memorabilia in connection with the Waverley line, which had a station here.

6 Return south on the B6357 and after Canonbie join the A7 to return to England through Longtown and Carlisle.

On the edge of Longtown, Arthuret church overlooks the site of an important battle in the 6th century AD. According to Welsh poems, 30,000 were slain on the field and the wizard Merlin (Myrddin) was driven to madness by the death of his lord Gwenddoleu here.

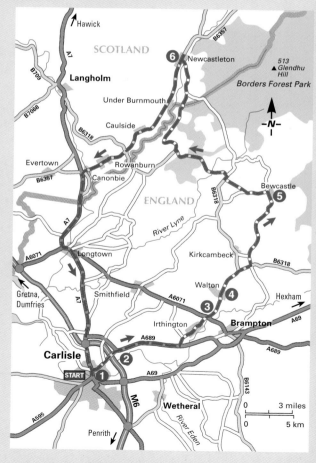

TOURIST INFORMATION CENTRES

Brampton
Moot Hall, Market Square.
Tel: 01697 73433

Carlisle
The Old Town Hall.
Tel: 01228 625600

Gretna
Gretna Outlet Village.
Tel: 01461 337834

PLACES OF INTEREST

Bewcastle Cross
Bewcastle. Free.

Birdoswald Roman Fort
Gilsland, near Carlisle.
Tel: 01697 747602
Dating from AD 125, the fort housed up to 500 Roman soldiers stationed on Hadrian's Wall. The perimeter wall, entrance gates and one turret can be seen. There is an interactive visitor centre on the site.

Border Regiment and King's Own Royal Border Regiment Museum
Queen Mary's Tower,
The Castle, Carlisle.
Tel: 01228 532774. Trophies, models, pictures and silver tell the story of the regiment.

Carlisle Castle
Castle Way, Carlisle.
Tel: 01228 591922
Medieval castle captured by Bonnie Prince Charlie in 1745. Houses a regimental museum (see above).

Carlisle Cathedral
Tel: 01228 548151;
www.carlislecathedral.org.uk
Founded in 1122, this handsome red sandstone church contains excellent stained glass and the Brougham Triptych – a 16th-century Flemish carved altarpiece.

Guildhall Museum
Green Market, Carlisle.
Tel: 01228 534781
Local history displays and the stories behind the Guilds.

Lanercost Priory
Tel: 01697 73030
Augustinian Priory in a delightful wooded valley 2 miles (3.2km) northeast of Brampton. The main priory buildings are in ruins, but the nave of the church survives and is now the local parish church.

Settle–Carlisle Railway
Scenic 72-mile (115.2km) route. For further details about the special steam trips which run occasionally along the line, as well as the standard trains, contact the local Tourist Information Centre or check the website www.settle-carlisle.co.uk.

Solway Aviation Museum
Carlisle Airport, Crosby-on-Eden. Tel: 01228 573823;
www.solway-aviation-museum.co.uk
Exhibits include a Vulcan bomber as well as remnants from Blue Streak, the failed missile project from nearby RAF Spadeadam.

Tullie House Museum and Art Gallery
Castle Street, Carlisle.
Tel: 01228 534781
Interactive displays trace the history of Carlisle, including on the Romans, the reivers, Robert the Bruce and the Roundheads.

SHOPPING

Brampton
Market, Wed.

Carlisle
Market, Mon to Sat.

LOCAL SPECIALITIES

Ice creams and sorbets
Cumbrian Cottage, Gelt House Farm, Hayton, Carlisle.
Tel: 01228 670296

Woollens
Linton Tweed Shop, Shaddongate, Carlisle.
Tel: 01228 527569

PERFORMING ARTS

Sands Centre
Carlisle. Tel: 01228 625222

Stanwix Arts Theatre
Brampton Road, Carlisle.
Tel: 01228 400356

■ OUTDOOR ACTIVITIES

ANGLING

New Mills Trout Farm, near Brampton. Tel: 01697 741115
Talkin Tarn Country Park. Tel: 01697 73129

CYCLE HIRE

Brampton

Pedal Pushers. Tel: 01697 742387

GOLF COURSES

Brampton

Brampton Golf Club. Tel: 01697 72255/72000

Carlisle

Carlisle Golf Club, Aglionby. Tel: 01228 513029
Stony Holme, St Aidans Road. Tel: 01228 625511

GUIDED WALKS

Carlisle

Guided city walks (summer only). Details from Carlisle Tourist Information Centre. Charge.

HORSE RACING

Carlisle Racecourse

Durdar Road. Tel: 01228 554700

HORSE-RIDING

Brampton

Bailey Mill Farm, near Roadhead. Tel: 01697 72384

Carlisle

Blackdyke Farm, Blackford. Tel: 01228 674633
Cargo Riding Centre, Cargo. Tel: 01228 674300
Stonerigg Riding Centre, The Bow, Great Orton. Tel: 01228 576232

LONG-DISTANCE FOOTPATHS & TRAILS

The Cumbria Way

Carlisle and Ulverston are linked by this 70-mile (113km) route through the Lake District.

Hadrian's Wall National Trail

England's most recent National Trail follows the Roman frontier for 84 miles (134km) from Bowness-on-Solway to Tyneside.

WATERSPORTS

Brampton

Talkin Tarn Country Park. Canoeing, rowing, sailing and windsurfing are available. Tel: 01697 73129

■ ANNUAL EVENTS & CUSTOMS

Bewcastle

Bewcastle Sports (including sheepdog trials), late Aug.

Brampton

Brampton Sheepdog Trials, mid-Sep.

Carlisle

Carlisle and Borders Spring Show, early May.
Carlisle Carnival, mid-Jun.
Cumberland Show, mid-Jul.

Tea Rooms

The Boathouse Café

Talkin Tarn, Brampton
CA8 1HN
Tel: 01697 741050
Upstairs from one of the tarn's boathouses, this welcoming café is the perfect place to reflect on the view and tuck into home-made cakes and hot chocolate. There's a little gift shop, too.

Garden Restaurant

Tullie House Museum and Art Gallery, Castle Street, Carlisle CA3 8TP
Tel: 01228 618718;
www.tulliehouse.co.uk
On the ground floor of the museum and art gallery, overlooking the quiet garden, this large refectory-style eatery is a great meeting place close to Carlisle's city centre. Serving snacks and more substantial lunches, it's also family friendly.

High Head Sculpture Valley Tearoom

High Head Farm, Ivegill
Carlisle CA4 0PJ
Tel: 01697 473552;
www.highheadsculpture
valley.co.uk
Jonathan and Bernadette Stamper created this peculiar artistic haven on a working farm and the tea room is the ideal place to start or end your visit to the sculpture park. The exquisite food is freshly prepared, much of it following original farmhouse recipes, and the outside seating area offers glimpses into the sculpture park itself.

Lanercost Tearooms

Abbey Farm, Lanercost, Brampton CA8 2HQ
Tel: 01697 741267
In the grounds of the 12th-century abbey, and just 0.25 miles (400m) from Hadrian's Wall, this delightful courtyard development includes a farm shop and craft gallery as well as an excellent tea room and restaurant. Home-made cakes and scones top off a menu that makes the most of locally grown ingredients.

Pubs

Belted Will

Hallbankgate, Brampton
Tel: 01697 746236;
www.beltedwill.co.uk
The 'Will' in question was Lord William Howard from nearby Naworth Castle, a feudal baron in the time of the Reivers. Today you'll find this award-winning village pub serves a very decent pint, alongside simple but well-delivered food such as Cumberland sausage or honey roast duck.

Pheasant Inn

Cumwhitton, Brampton
CA4 9EX Tel: 01228 560102
The Pheasant has built an enviable reputation both for the quality of its food, and of its cask ales, which are drawn from a range of local breweries and from further afield. It's certainly worth seeking out from amid the tangle of quiet lanes that typify this rural backwater.

Blacksmiths Arms

Talkin, Brampton CA8 1LE
Tel: 01697 73452;
www.blacksmithstalkin.co.uk
Facing the green in this picturesque Pennine fellside village, the Blacksmith's serves à la carte in a small restaurant or simpler fare in the lounge bars. There's always a range of cask ales available and accommodation can be booked in the inn.

Plough Inn

Wreay, Carlisle CA4 0RL
Tel: 01697 475770;
www.wreayplough.co.uk
The village is famous for its peculiar church, designed in the 19th century by Sarah Losh. The pub serves excellent local beers, including Hesket Newmarket and Geltsdale, alongside good food prepared from locally sourced ingredients.

■ LAKE DISTRICT NATIONAL PARK INFORMATION POINTS

KENDAL, WINDERMERE & KENT ESTUARY

Elterwater
Maple Tree Corner Shop.

Far Sawrey
The Post Office.

Rusland
Forest Spinners.

ESKDALE & WASDALE

Boot
The Post Office.

Ravenglass
Ravenglass and Eskdale
Railway Station.

Ulpha
Ulpha Post Office, Duddon
Valley, Broughton-in-Furness.

Wasdale Head
Barn Door Shop.

WESTERN LAKES

Ennerdale
Ennerdale Bridge Post Office.

Gosforth
Gosforth Pottery.

High Lorton
The Post Office.

St Bees
The Post Office, 122 Main
Street.

ULLSWATER, PENRITH & EASTERN FELLS

Bampton
Bampton Post Office.

■ OTHER INFORMATION

Cumbria Wildlife Trust
Plumgarths, Crook Road,
Kendal. Tel: 01539 816300;
www.wildlifetrust.org.uk

English Heritage
Canada House, 3 Chepstow
Street, Manchester.
Tel: 0161 242 1400;
www.english-heritage.org.uk

Forestry Commission
Grizedale Forest Visitor
Centre, Grizedale,
Hawkshead, Ambleside.
Tel: 01229 860010

**Lake District National Park
Authority Headquarters**
Murley Moss,
Oxenholme Road, Kendal.
Tel: 01539 724555;
www.lake-district.gov.uk

National Trust in Cumbria
The Hollens, Grasmere,
Ambleside, Cumbria.
Tel: 0870 609 5391;
www.nationaltrust.org.uk

Parking
Information on parking
permits and car parks is
available from local TICs.

Public Transport
The Traveline service gives
details of buses, boats, trains
and ferries operating
throughout Cumbria.
Tel: 0871 2002 233

Weather
Lake District Weather
Service. Tel: 0844 846 2444

Places of Interest
There will be an admission
charge unless otherwise
stated. We give details of just
some of the facilities within
the area covered by this
guide. Further information
can be obtained from local
TICs or online.

Angling
Numerous opportunities for
fishing on farms, lakes and
rivers. Permits and licences
are available from local tackle
shops and TICs.

■ ORDNANCE SURVEY MAPS

KENDAL, WINDERMERE & KENT ESTUARY
Landranger 1:50,000;
Sheets 96, 97
Explorer OL 1:25,000;
Sheets 6, 7

ESKDALE & WASDALE
Landranger 1:50,000;
Sheets 89, 95
Explorer OL: 1:25,000; Sheet 6

WESTERN LAKES
Landranger 1:50,000; Sheet 89
Explorer OL 1:25,000; Sheet 4

BASSENTHWAITE & BORROWDALE
Landranger 1:50,000;
Sheets 85, 89
Explorer OL 1:25,000; Sheet 4

ULLSWATER, PENRITH & EASTERN FELLS
Landranger 1:50,000;
Sheets 90, 91
Explorer OL 1:25,000;
Sheets 5, 7, 19, 43

CARLISLE & BORDERLANDS
Landranger 1:50,000; Sheet 85
Explorer 1:25,000;
Sheets 314, 315, 324,
Explorer OL 1:25,000; Sheet 43

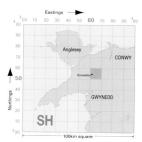

The National Grid system covers Great Britain with an imaginary network of grid squares. Each is 100km square in area and is given a unique alphabetic reference, as shown in the diagram above.

These squares are sub-divided into one hundred 10km squares, identified by vertical lines (eastings) and horizontal lines (northings). The reference for the square a feature is located within is made by adding the numbers of the two lines which cross in the bottom left corner of that square to the alphabetic reference (ignoring the small figures). The easting is quoted first. For example, SH6050.

For a 2-figure reference, the zeros are omitted, giving just SH65. In this book, we use 4-figure references, which allow us to pinpoint the feature more accurately by dividing the 10km square into one hundred 1km squares. These squares are not actually printed on the road atlas but are estimated by eye. The same process is carried out as before, giving an enhanced reference of SH6154.

Key to Atlas

Symbol	Description		Symbol	Description
M4	Motorway with number		Toll	Toll
S Fleet	Motorway service area			Road under construction
	Motorway toll			Narrow Primary route with passing places
	Motorway junction with and without number			Steep gradient
	Restricted motorway junctions			Railway station and level crossing
	Motorway and junction under construction			Tourist railway
A3	Primary route single/dual carriageway			National trail
BATH	Primary route destinations			Forest drive
	Roundabout			Heritage coast
Y 5 Y	Distance in miles between symbols			Ferry route
A1123	Other A Road single/dual carriageway	6	Walk start point
B2070	B road single/dual carriageway	1	Cycle start point
	Unclassified road single/dual carriageway	3	Tour start point
	Road tunnel			

Symbol	Description		Symbol	Description
⌂	Abbey, cathedral or priory	NTS	National Trust for Scotland property
	Aquarium		Nature reserve
	Castle	★	Other place of interest
	Cave	P+R	Park and Ride location
	Country park		Picnic site
	County cricket ground		Steam centre
	Farm or animal centre		Ski slope natural
	Garden		Ski slope artifical
	Golf course		
	Historic house	i	Tourist Information Centre
	Horse racing		Viewpoint
	Motor racing	V	Visitor or heritage centre
	Museum		Zoological or wildlife collection
	Airport		Forest Park
	Heliport		National Park (England & Wales)
	Windmill		
NT	National Trust property		National Scenic Area (Scotland)

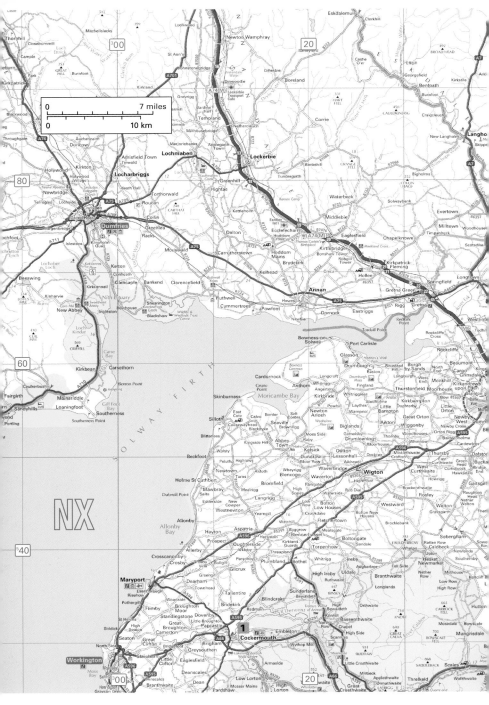

The Automobile Association would like to thank the following photographers and companies for their assistance in the preparation of this book. Abbreviations for the picture credits are as follows – (t) top; (b) bottom; (c) centre; (l) left; (r) right; (AA) AA World Travel Library

1 Anna Stowe Landscapes UK/Alamy; 4/5 AA/Tom Mackie; 8t Tony West/www.cumbriaphoto.co.uk; 8b AA/Steve Day; 9 AA/Tom Mackie; 10t AA/Tom Mackie; 10c AA/Steve Day; 10b Val Corbet/www.cumbriaphoto.co.uk; 11t AA/Tom Mackie; 11b AA/Steve Day; 13 Julian Marshall/Alamy; 14tl AA/E A Bowness; 14tr Laurie Campbell; 14b AA/Tom Mackie; 18-19 AA/Tom Mackie; 21t AA/Pete Bennett; 21b AA/Steve Day; 22 AA/Steve Day; 23t AA/E A Bowness; 23b AA/Steve Day; 26 Jason Smalley/Wildscape/Alamy; 35 AA/Tom Mackie; 41 AA/Tom Mackie; 46 AA/Tom Mackie; 48-49 AA/Tom Mackie; 51t AA/AA/Jon Sparks; 51b AA/Tom Mackie; 52 AA/Jon Sparks; 53t AA/Jon Sparks; 53c AA/Tom Mackie; 53b AA/Tom Mackie; 55 AA/E A Bowness; 60 Neil Barks/ Alamy; 65 AA/Tom Mackie; 68 AA/Jon Sparks; 70-71 CW Images/Alamy; 73 AA/Peter Sharpe; 74 AA/Tom Mackie; 75t Mark Glaister/StockShot/Alamy; 75b Ashley Cooper/Alamy; 77 AA/Tom Mackie; 85 AA/E A Bowness; 90 AA/Jon Sparks; 92-93 AA/Steve Day; 95 AA/Steve Day; 96c AA/Steve Day; 96/97 AA/Tom Mackie; 97t AA/Peter Sharpe; 97c AA/Steve Day; 99 AA/Tom Mackie; 104 AA/Tom Mackie; 110 AA/Steve Day; 112-113 AA/Steve Day; 115tl AA/Tom Mackie; 115tr AA/E A Bowness; 115b AA/E A Bowness; 116 AA/Tom Mackie; 117t John Morrison/Alamy; 117c AA/Steve Day; 117b AA/Peter Sharpe; 120 AA/E A Bowness; 127 Ed Rhodes/Alamy; 134 AA/Jon Sparks; 136-137 AA/Roger Coulam; 139tl AA/Roger Coulam; 139tr AA/Roger Coulam; 139b Graeme Peacock/Alamy; 140t AA/Roger Coulam; 140b AA/Roger Coulam; 141t AA/Roger Coulam; 141c AA/Roger Coulam;141b AA/Roger Coulam; 145 Walter Bibikow/Getty Images; 150 AA/Roger Coulam.